D1372294

AMERICAN HISTORY:

From Colonial Times to the 21st Century

**DARNLEY
PUBLISHING
GROUP**

Legal deposit – Bibliothèque et Archives nationales du Québec, 2009
Legal deposit – Library and Archives Canada, 2009

ISBN 978-2-923623-51-1

Printed in Canada

Catalog number: TBCD8

Author:
Krista E. Garver

Editor-In-Chief:
Claude Major, Ph.D.

Project Manager:
Francine Hebert, M.Ed.

Design and Cover:
Rasha Razzak

American History: From Colonial Times to the 21st Century

> *No great man lives in vain. The history of the world is but the biography of great men.*
>
> THOMAS CARLYLE
> 1795–1881

INTRODUCTION

Compared with many other countries in the world, the United States has had a very short history. Yet, in that brief period of time, Americans have been very busy! From the moment the United States declared its independence from Britain, Americans have done much to contribute to the development of the modern world. In the late 1700s, the Founding Fathers of the United States created a system of self-government that would serve as a model to many parts of the world in their quest for democracy. Now, in the early part of the twenty-first century, American knowledge and innovation are behind many breakthroughs in scientific research, American authors and artists are prominent on the international scene, and American politicians and activists work to improve conditions for people around the globe.

In order to participate fully in the democratic American society, it is important to understand how the United States has developed into the nation that it is today, with all of its achievements, its problems, its successes, and its failures. American culture, society, people, and politics are constantly evolving, and the United States of today has its roots in events that happened ten, twenty, or even a couple of hundred years ago. Understanding these roots can help us to better understand and deal with the problems and issues that arise all the time in modern America. Having a firm grasp on the past allows us to interpret the present and look forward to the future.

This book is organized according to themes that make the United States unique. Chapter 1 examines the various peoples from around the world who came together to make up American society; chapter 2 reviews the early history of the country through the many armed conflicts in which it has participated; chapter 3 provides mini biographical accounts of some of the country's greatest presidents and political leaders; chapter 4 briefly explains the system of government and how it has evolved; chapter 5 focuses on the major events that have taken place since the end of World War II; and chapter 6 introduces several notable Americans who have made long-lasting contributions to the development of the nation.

CHAPTER ONE

WHO Are We?

A country is defined by its borders and geographic location, but much more so by its people. The roots of American identity can be traced from the early migration of Paleo-Indians to twentieth-century immigration trends.

THE LINCOLN MEMORIAL

Architect Henry Bacon modeled his design for the building after the Greek Parthenon. Built into the design are symbols such as the thirty-six exterior Doric columns representing the thirty-six states in the Union at the time of Lincoln's death. Those states are listed on the frieze above the columns. Above those states are listed the forty-eight states in the Union when the memorial was built, making the memorial a tribute to the Union as much as a tribute to Lincoln himself. Alaska and Hawaii are represented with a plaque on the front steps.

*America is God's Crucible, the great Melting-Pot
where all the races of Europe are melting and reforming!*
ISRAEL ZANGWILL
1864–1926

The United States has always been a nation of immigrants, a *melting pot* where people of different ethnicities all come together to form a new identity: American. Although in practice many immigrants have faced various kinds of discrimination (racial, ethnic, religious, etc.), in theory this is a country where anyone can build a new life and pursue the American Dream. We will begin this text by looking at the variety of people who have settled in America throughout its history, and whose descendents to this day make up the rich fabric of American society.

NATIVE AMERICANS

More than 500 years ago, when the first Europeans took up residence in what is now the United States, the land became known as the New World. Prior to that time, many people thought that there was nothing beyond Europe, Asia, and Africa. However, there were people in America long before the arrival of the first Europeans; indeed, it had already been populated for close to 15,000 years.

There are a couple of theories about how the first human beings came to America, and no one knows exactly when

it happened, but evidence suggests that they arrived by crossing what is now the Bering Strait. It is thought that at the end of the most recent Ice Age, a stretch of land, called a land bridge, was exposed between Alaska and Siberia, and that the first people, the Paleo-Indians, simply walked across it (though with the harsh climate, there was probably nothing simple about it!). From there, the travelers radiated southward and eastward, eventually dividing into small groups that evolved their own languages and cultures. These people are the ancestors of present-day Native Americans, or American Indians. Based on similarities and differences among the Indian languages, it is estimated that there were three distinct waves of immigration across the land bridge, and it is thought that there were several million Native Americans living on the continent before the first European settlers arrived.

Native American tribes were originally migratory hunter-gatherer societies— they followed the movement of big game animals, such as buffalo and moose, and gathered fruits and nuts. There is evidence that as early as 4,000 B.C., some Native American tribes started domesticating some animals and crops, so that rather than moving along with the herds, they were living in small farming communities. They raised animals such as turkeys and dogs, and grew a variety of crops including pumpkins, sweet potatoes, and maize (Indian corn).

Native peoples across North and South America developed unique and advanced societies, and their cultures became as different from each other as American culture is from Mexican culture. For example, the Apaches were known for their savagery in war; the Hopis were known for being peaceful. Some tribes made their mark through works of art, such as the Indians in the Pacific Northwest who created totem poles and the Anasazis who are known for their beautiful baskets and pottery. The illustration on page 7 provides a brief summary of the names of tribes and the main areas occupied by Native Americans in what is now the United States and Canada. (Note: this list is far from complete.)

EUROPEAN SETTLERS AND AFRICAN SLAVES

When Christopher Columbus sailed from Spain in 1492, he was trying to reach Asia, and when he landed in what is now the Bahamas, he thought he had found it. Although Columbus had not found a convenient water passage to Asia, he had found a land previously unknown to the rest of the world. For about the next 100 years, explorers from many countries in Europe led many voyages to find ways to

Twenty African slaves were brought to Jamestown, Virginia, in 1619. A series of complex colonial laws began to relegate Africans and their descendants to slavery. The United States outlawed the transatlantic slave trade in 1808, but slavery continued until 1865.

exploit this newly discovered region. By the end of the sixteenth century, Spain had established cities in what would become Florida and New Mexico, and France had claimed some land farther west. The first permanent British settlement in America was Jamestown, Virginia, in 1607. Many more settlements took root in the next several years as people left Europe seeking adventure, religious freedom, and business opportunities, among other reasons.

NATIVE INDIAN REGIONAL ORIGINS

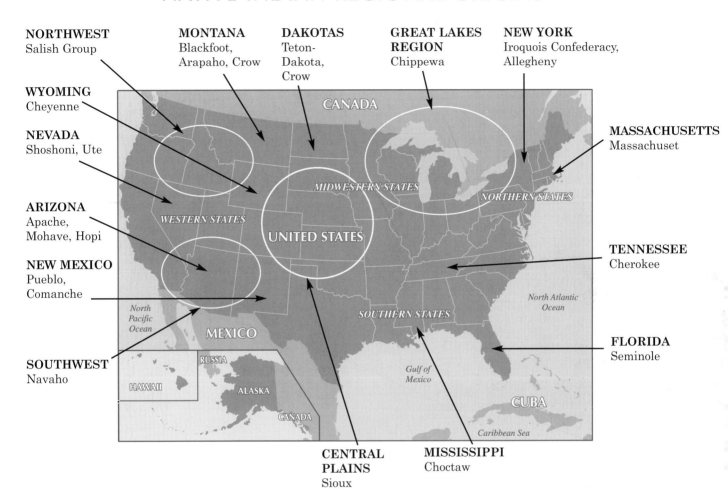

NORTHWEST
Salish Group

MONTANA
Blackfoot,
Arapaho, Crow

DAKOTAS
Teton-
Dakota,
Crow

**GREAT LAKES
REGION**
Chippewa

NEW YORK
Iroquois Confederacy,
Allegheny

WYOMING
Cheyenne

NEVADA
Shoshoni, Ute

ARIZONA
Apache,
Mohave, Hopi

NEW MEXICO
Pueblo,
Comanche

SOUTHWEST
Navaho

MASSACHUSETTS
Massachuset

TENNESSEE
Cherokee

FLORIDA
Seminole

**CENTRAL
PLAINS**
Sioux

MISSISSIPPI
Choctaw

Canadian Band Origins:

Inuit — broadly distributed across northern and northeastern territories; Mi'kmaq — Maritime provinces; Mohawk — Quebec, Ontario, and south into New York; Huron — Quebec, Ontario, and south into Ohio Valley; Ojibwa — Ontario and Manitoba; Cree — Quebec and west to Alberta; Blackfoot — Alberta

People from the Netherlands, Scotland, and Ireland also set up settlements in the area during this time.

The first record of Africans being brought to the New World is from 1619, when twenty black indentured servants arrived on a Dutch ship. An indentured servant was someone who had a debt to pay and signed a contract to work off that debt over a period of between three and seven years. There were many indentured servants in the New World, mostly poor white Europeans working off the price of their passage to America. After the settlers had tried many types of farming, tobacco became the main crop, particularly in the southern regions. Tobacco is quite labor intensive, and landowners soon discovered the benefit to having servants that they didn't have to pay; thus, more and more Africans were bought or kidnapped from their home countries. More than 600,000 Africans are thought to have been brought to America during that time. In 1705, the colony of Virginia sealed the fate of these workers by passing the first Slave Codes, which defined slaves as property rather than people. The Codes also described punishments to be doled out to slaves who committed crimes (including such offenses as associating with whites), and stated that masters could take any steps necessary to punish slaves, even if the end result was death. Slave Codes were subsequently passed by the remaining colonies, and it would take another 160 years for slavery to be abolished in the country.

WAVES OF IMMIGRATION

Following the Revolutionary War which established the United States of America (see chapter 2), there were several waves of immigration. As during the initial settling of the New World, people from many countries came for many reasons.

In the early 1800s, due to a famine in their homeland, about one-half the population of Ireland immigrated to the United States. Because most of them were poor and could not buy land, they tended to settle in the major cities. In the middle of the century, there were also large groups of Germans who moved to America. They came mainly because of political unrest and revolution; many were exiled, and other countries were unwilling to except German immigrants. Unlike the Irish, most Germans had the money to purchase land, and many settled in areas of the Midwest. These two groups of people did not always get along very well, partly because of religious opposition—the Irish were Protestant, the Germans were Roman Catholic—and partly because of political opposition.

In the mid-nineteenth century, gold was discovered in California, which brought even more people seeking their fortunes. Chinese immigrants started arriving to prospect for gold and to work on the transcontinental railroad. They were mostly manual laborers and faced an extreme amount of discrimination and prejudice, often because their language and culture were so different from those of the European immigrants. In 1882 Congress passed the Chinese Exclusion Act, which (along with a series of subsequent laws) restricted Chinese immigration for close to a century.

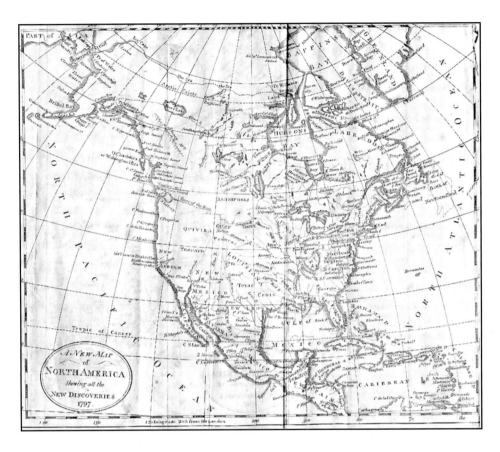

This original map appeared in The American Gazetter published by Jedidiah Morse in 1797. The map was specially engraved for the country's first geographical dictionary.

Around the turn of the century (roughly 1880–1920), there was another large influx of people to the United States, including French Canadians, Italians, Scandinavians, Russians, and Japanese. Jewish immigrants also arrived in large quantities. Coming from Germany, Syria, Eastern Europe, and elsewhere, more than 2 million Jews entered the country, mainly fleeing from discrimination and oppression in their homelands. As opposed to earlier years, when most immigrants were welcomed, the people coming during this later wave of immigration were often feared and despised by those who were already here. For one thing, many Americans were afraid that immigrants would take over their jobs. In addition, the customs and lifestyles of Russians and Japanese, for example, were much different from those of the English and other Western Europeans who had originally settled in the country.

The following decades, encompassing the Great Depression and World War II, saw relatively little immigration to the United

States. In 1965, Congress overhauled immigration law to emphasize reuniting families and attracting skilled laborers and professionals. As a result, the numbers of Asian and Mexican immigrants have increased significantly in recent years.

The information given here is not exhaustive. Smaller groups of people have also come to the United States seeking refugee status or fleeing political turmoil in their home countries. For example, in 1956 many Hungarians came following a revolution in Hungary, and in the 1960s many Cubans immigrated due to political upheaval in Cuba. Some groups have also come following wars between the U.S. and their home countries (for example, many Filipinos immigrated after the U.S. annexed the Philippines in 1898).

There have always been a great many more people wanting to come to the U.S. than could be absorbed socially or economically, and in 1790 Congress started passing laws either restricting or easing restrictions on immigration. The relative openness to increasing or decreasing the numbers of immigrants varies depending on the current political, economic, and social conditions in the country. However, it is doubtful that the United States will ever close its doors entirely to the people who dream of participating in American society, with its freedom and potential for prosperity and personal achievement. America was built through the dedication and labor of immigrants of all races and ethnicities, and the country continues to be defined by the diversity of peoples and cultures that choose to make the United States their home.

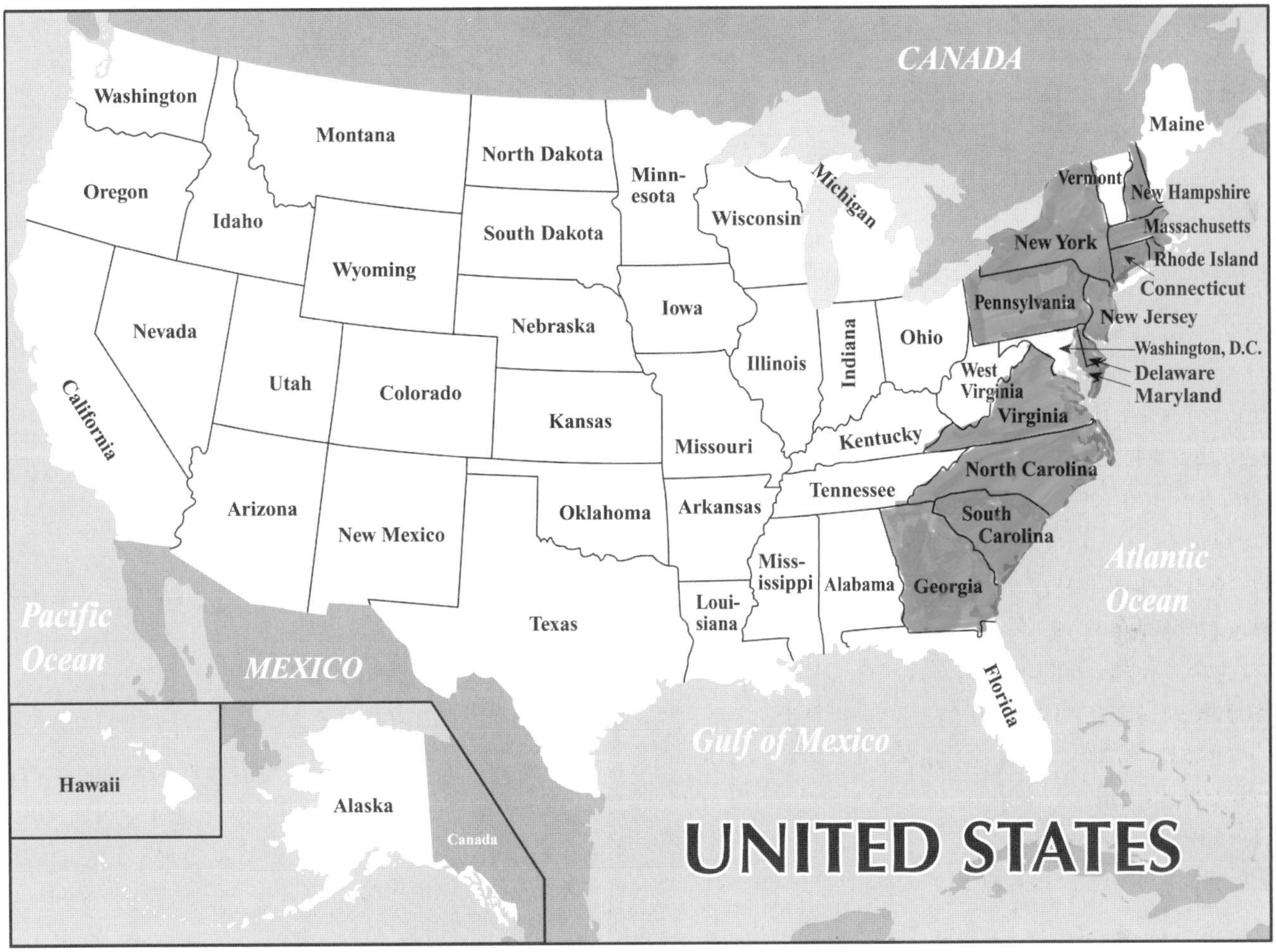
CANADA
Washington
Montana
North Dakota
Minn-
esota
Michigan
Maine
Vermont
New Hampshire
Oregon
Idaho
South Dakota
Wisconsin
Massachusetts
New York
Rhode Island
Wyoming
Connecticut
Pennsylvania
Iowa
New Jersey
Nevada
Nebraska
Ohio
Indiana
Illinois
Washington, D.C.
Delaware
West
Virginia
Maryland
Utah
Colorado
California
Virginia
Kansas
Kentucky
Missouri
North Carolina
Tennessee
Arizona
Oklahoma
Arkansas
South
Carolina
New Mexico
Atlantic
Ocean
Miss-
issippi
Alabama
Georgia
Pacific
Ocean
Texas
Loui-
siana
MEXICO
Florida
Gulf of Mexico
Hawaii
Alaska
Canada
UNITED STATES

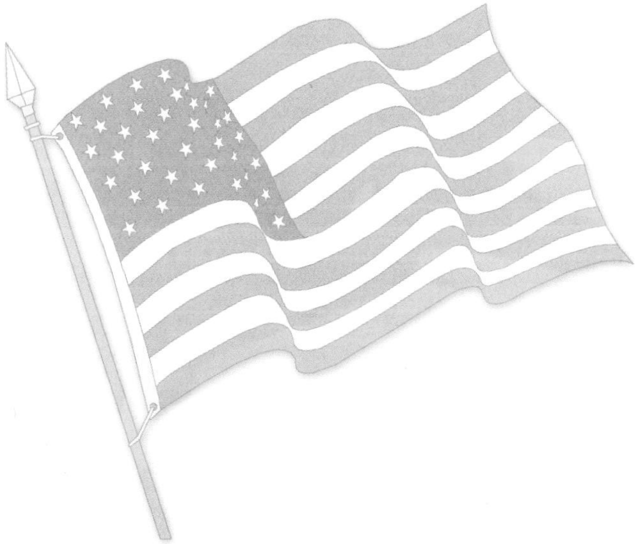

★ Daniels, Roger. *Coming to America: A History of Immigration and Ethnicity in American Life, 2nd edition.* New York: Harper Perennial, 2002.

★ Gabaccia, Donna. *Immigration and American Diversity: A Social and Cultural History.* Malden, Massachusetts: Blackwell Publishers, 2002.

★ Jacobson, Matthew Frye. *Whiteness of a Different Color: European Immigrants and the Alchemy of Race.* Cambridge, Massachusetts: Harvard University Press, 1988.

★ King, Desmond. *Making Americans: Immigration, Race, and the Origins of the Diverse Democracy.* Cambridge, Massachusetts: Harvard University Press, 2002.

★ Rediker, Marcus. *The Slave Ship: A Human History.* New York: Viking Penguin, 2007.

1. Which present-day American state was probably first visited by Paleo-Indians who took the land bridge route to North America?

2. Name a group of North American Indians who are primarily associated with the Great Lakes area.

3. What was the first permanent British settlement in the New World?

4. Which group of immigrants was particularly instrumental in building the western portion of the transcontinental railroad?

5. In what year were the first Africans brought to America?

ANSWERS TO QUIZ ONE

1- Alaska   2- Chippewa   3- Jamestown, Virginia   4- Chinese   5- 1619

AMERICA
at War

From its birth by revolution to the complex lessons of Vietnam and the Persian Gulf, America has a history that is marked by war.

ARLINGTON NATIONAL CEMETERY

Arlington National Cemetery, a United States federal burial ground in northeastern Virginia, was designated a military cemetery in 1864. The site, on the Potomac River across from Washington, D.C., occupies more than 612 acres and contains the remains of more than 300,000 veterans, political leaders, and their spouses.

The use of force alone is but temporary. It may subdue for a moment; but it does not remove the necessity of subduing again; and a nation is not governed, which is perpetually to be conquered.

EDMUND BURKE
1729–1797

Victory at all costs, victory in spite of terror, victory however long and hard the road may be; for without victory there is no survival.

SIR WINSTON CHURCHILL
1874–1965

There never was a good war or a bad peace.

BENJAMIN FRANKLIN
1706–1790

Starting with the war that led to the birth of the United States of America, the country has participated in many armed conflicts, both at home and abroad.

This chapter provides an overview of the various wars that have shaped American history.

★ The Revolutionary War

★ The War of 1812

★ The Indian Wars

★ The Mexican–American War

★ The Civil War

★ The Spanish–American War

★ World War I

★ World War II

★ The Korean War

★ The Vietnam War

★ The Persian Gulf War

★ The War in Afghanistan

★ The Iraq War

THE REVOLUTIONARY WAR AND THE BIRTH OF A NATION

1764	1765	1766	1767	1773	1774	1775	1776	1781	1783
Sugar Act	Quartering Act / Stamp Act	Declaratory Act	Beginning of Townshend Acts	Tea Act / Boston Tea Party	Intolerable Acts / First Continental Congress	War begins at Lexington	Second Continental Congress / Declaration of Independence	Cornwallis surrenders at Yorktown	Treaty of Paris signed

In 1607, King James I of England granted a charter to a London investment company to establish a British colony in Jamestown, Virginia. Over the next roughly 150 years, many more people would cross the Atlantic to set up new homes in North America. By about 1750, there were British colonies spanning the east coast of the continent, from Newfoundland in the north to Honduras in the south, including thirteen in what is now the United States of America. The colonists came to the New World for many reasons—some seeking business opportunities, some fleeing religious persecution, and so on.

The Revolutionary War between the colonists and the British began in 1775, though tensions had been building for more than a decade. For most of the period leading up to the war, there was relatively little conflict between the groups—the colonists were British citizens and were perfectly happy to live under British rule. The colonies had an abundance of resources and provided an economic boost for England through trade. In return, the colonists enjoyed higher wages than many of their European counterparts, they had their own local legislatures, and the few taxes that existed were not very well enforced. In essence, the colonists were pretty much left alone.

Britain was not the only European country to establish colonies in North America, and between 1754 and 1763, Britain and France were involved in a major conflict to establish dominance in the New World. The British won, and their victory was much celebrated by the colonists, who saw a great opportunity to expand westward. They started to get a feeling of foreboding, however, when the

No *Stamped* Paper to be had.

B O S T O N, *October 28.*

WE hear from Halifax, in the province of Nova-Scotia, that on Sunday, the 13th inft. in the morning, was difcovered hanging on the gallows behind the Citadel Hill, the effigies of a ftampman, accompanied with a boot and devil, together with labels fuitable to the occafion (which we cannot infert, not being favoured with the fame) this we are informed gave great pleafure and fatisfaction to all the friends of liberty and their country there, as they hope from this inftance of their zeal, the neighbouring colonies will be charitable enough to believe that nothing but their dependent fituation, prevents them from heartily and fincerely oppofing a tax unconftitutional in its nature, and of fo deftructive a tendency as muft infallibly entail poverty and beggary on us and our pofterity, if carried in execution.

On the 23d inftant the Great and General Court met here, according to adjournment; and we hear that almoft every member of the honourable houfe of reprefentatives have received inftructions from their conftituents; and that they are of the fame import with thofe already publifhed.

We hear that the merchants and friends to America in England, were determined to ufe their utmoft endeavours the next feffion of Parliament, in order to get the ftamp act repealed.

N E W - Y O R K, *November 4.*

The late extraordinary and unprecedented preparations in Fort George, and the fecuring of the ftamped paper in that garrifon, having greatly alarmed and difpleafed the inhabitants of this city, a vaft number of them affembled laft Friday evening in the commons, from whence they marched down the Fly (preceded by a number of lights) and having ftopped a few minutes at the Coffeehoufe, proceeded to the Fort walls, where they broke open the ftable of the L------t G------r, took out his coach, and after carrying the fame through the principal ftreets of the city, in triumph marched to the commons, where a gallows was erected :

George the Third, to the crown of Great-Britain, &c. upon which occafion the faid freemen unanimoufly, and with one voice declared, Firft. That they have at all times heretofore, and ever would bear true allegiance to his Majefty King George the Third, and his royal predeceffors, and wifhed to be governed agreeable to the laws of the land, and the Britifh conftitution, to which they ever had, and for ever moft chearfully would fubmit.

Secondly. That the ftamp act, prepared for the Britifh colonies in America, in their opinion, is unconftitutional; and fhould the fame take place, agreeable to the tenor of it, would be a manifeft deftruction and overthrow of their long enjoyed, boafted and invaluable liberties and privileges.

Thirdly. That they will, by all lawful ways and means, endeavour to preferve and tranfmit to pofterity, their liberty and property, in as full and ample manner as they received the fame from their anceftors.

Fourthly. That they will difcountenance and difcourage, by all lawful meafures, the execution and effect of the ftamp act.

Fifthly. That they will deteft, abhor, and hold in the utmoft contempt, all and every perfon or perfons, who fhall meanly accept of any employment or office, relating to the ftamp act, or fhall take any fhelter or advantage from the fame; and all and every ftamp pimp, informer, favourer and encourager of the execution of the faid act; and that they will have no communication with any fuch perfon, nor fpeak to them on any occafion, unlefs it be to inform them of their vilenefs.

C I T Y of N E W - Y O R K, *October 31, 1765.*

AT a general Meeting of the Merchants of the City of New-York, trading to Great-Britain, at the Houfe of Mr. George Burns, of the faid City, Innholder, to confider what was neceffary to be done in the prefent Situation of Affairs, with refpect to the STAMP ACT, and the melancholy State of the North-American Commerce, fo greatly reftricted by the Impofitions and Duties eftablifhed by the late Acts of Trade: They came to the following Refolutions, viz.

First, That in all Orders they fend out to Great-Britain, for Goods or Merchandize, of any Nature, Kind or Quality whatfoever, ufually imported from Great-Britain, they will direct their Correfpondents not to fhip them, unlefs the STAMP ACT be repealed: It is neverthelefs agreed, that all fuch Merchants as are Owners of, and have Veffels already gone, and now cleared out for Great-Britain, fhall be at Liberty to bring back in them, on their own Accounts, Crates and Cafks of

Nov. 7, 1765, issue no. 1924, of the Pennsylvania Gazette, printed at Philadelphia by David Hall and Benjamin Franklin; without date, number, masthead, or imprint. On Oct. 31, 1765, the publishers announced the suspension of the Gazette in opposition to the provisions of the Stamp Act, which required that newspapers be printed on imported, stamped paper. By issuing sheets without the characteristic appearance of the newspaper they were able to satisfy the subscribers while protecting the firm from legal repercussions.

British royal Proclamation of 1763 set land boundaries, essentially prohibiting them from moving into the rich lands of the Ohio Valley. The colonists did not launch much of a protest against this proclamation, but seeds of bad blood between Britain and its colonial subjects were starting to be sewn.

Although Britain had won the war against France, it had also racked up a huge debt. Since much of the fighting had been to protect colonial land, the British government decided that the colonies should help pay for their own defense and, starting in 1764, passed a series of laws to raise revenue for the cause. Unfortunately for Britain, these laws were not looked upon favorably by the colonists, and eventually led to the beginnings of the American Revolution.

In 1764, the British Parliament passed the Sugar Act, which imposed a tax on coffee, sugar, molasses, and other products. In 1765, Parliament passed the Quartering Act requiring the colonies to house and supply British soldiers, and the Stamp Act placing a tax on all legal documents and publications including newspapers. As mentioned earlier, the colonists were British citizens; thus, they did not object to being governed by the British Parliament. However, since the colonists did not actually have any representation in Parliament, they did object to being taxed by it. These measures might have been more acceptable if it weren't for the fact that after the war the colonies (along with other parts of the world) entered a recession, causing the taxes to be viewed as particularly oppressive. The colonists

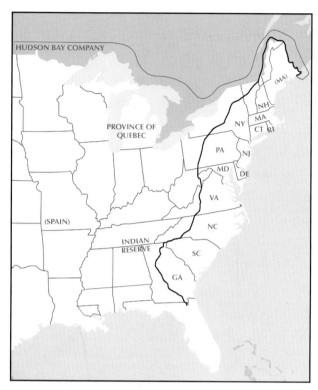

The original thirteen colonies of the United States

reacted by passing resolutions against the Stamp Act in their legislatures, and in a few instances there were violent protests.

In 1766, the British Parliament repealed the Stamp Act; however, it also passed the Declaratory Act, asserting its right to legislate for the colonies. The situation started to get out of hand in 1767, when Parliament began passing the Townshend Acts. Among other things, these laws imposed port taxes on several goods that the colonists could legally import only from Britain, including tea and paper. Violent protests again ensued, this time leading to a conflict between colonists and British troops in Boston Harbor in which five colonists were killed and six wounded. This incident, known as the Boston Massacre, proved to be

a significant foreshadowing of future events. Ironically enough, on the same day of the Boston Massacre, the British Parliament voted to repeal the taxes imposed by the Townshend Acts, all except for the tax on tea. This decision would doubtless haunt them in the years to come.

The British East India Company was a hugely influential trade venture that, due to an economic downturn in the post-war period, was hovering on the brink of bankruptcy in the 1770s. To avoid this potential catastrophe, Parliament passed several measures, one of which was designed to give the company a monopoly on the tea that could be shipped and distributed to the colonies. This law was known as the Tea Act of 1773. The combination of taxation and a trade monopoly proved too much for the colonists (particularly those in the rebellious city of Boston), and on December 16, 1773, several of them climbed onto a ship in Boston Harbor and threw about 90,000 pounds of tea into the water. This act came to be known as the Boston Tea Party.

Naturally, this act of defiance (not to mention the destruction of public property) could not go unpunished, and in 1774 Parliament passed the Coercive Acts, closing the port in Boston until the colonists paid for the tea and overturning the charter for Massachusetts, essentially taking over the colony. In all, there were four Coercive Acts which, along with the Quebec Act (providing support for French law and the Catholic Church in the north), came to be known in America as the Intolerable Acts. In the face

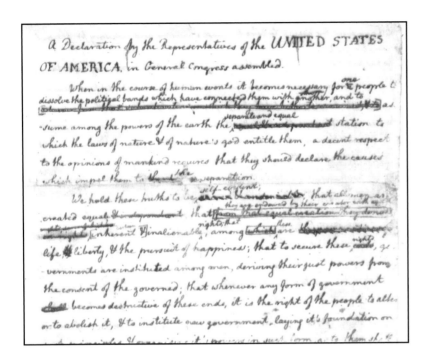

The "original Rough draught" of the Declaration of Independence, one of the great milestones in American history, shows the evolution of the text from the initial "fair copy" draft by Thomas Jefferson to the final text adopted by Congress on the morning of July 4, 1776. (See appendix C.)

of what they saw as British oppression, residents of the various colonies started to work together, and in 1774 representatives from twelve of the thirteen colonies (Georgia excluded) gathered in Philadelphia for the First Continental Congress. At this meeting, the delegates decided to bypass Parliament and appeal directly to the King of England. They resolved to meet again the next year if their grievances were not addressed.

Meanwhile, many of the colonies had been working to establish independent militias. These were not trained soldiers, but members of the community who were ready to fight if necessary at a moment's notice; thus, they were known as *minutemen.* The militia in Massachusetts had amassed a weapons cache in Concord, and since the colony was known for its revolutionary tendencies, in 1775 a British general ordered several hundred

of his men to destroy the weapons. The colonists learned about the plan, however, and when the British army reached Lexington, they were met by seventy-seven members of a local militia. The minutemen were outnumbered by about ten to one. It remains a mystery which side fired first, but in the end a handful of militiamen were killed and injured, and the British army pressed on to Concord. On the way, they were met by several bigger militias and were eventually forced to retreat back to Boston. However the fighting began, the Battles of Lexington and Concord officially signaled the start of the Revolutionary War.

Shortly after the Battles of Lexington and Concord, delegates from all thirteen colonies gathered for the Second Continental Congress to deal with the war. They organized the Continental Army and

Cornwallis and the British Army surrendered on October 19, 1781, in Yorktown, Virginia.

appointed General George Washington as its commander-in-chief. The Continental Army was in no way ready for a full-scale confrontation and the beginnings of the war were rough. The British soldiers, or *redcoats*, were well-supplied professionals led by General Charles Cornwallis; the Continental Army was a poor man's army— the soldiers lacked adequate clothing, shelter, and food, which was especially demoralizing during the winter months.

In many ways, the Revolutionary War was also a civil war between colonists who were fighting for America (patriots) and those who stayed loyal to Britain (loyalists). Even after the war broke out, many colonists saw reconciliation as the goal; they were fighting for their rights as British citizens, not for independence. As the war continued, however, reconciliation seemed less and less possible, and in 1776 the Second Continental Congress adopted the Declaration of Independence stating the intention of the colonies to be free from the British Empire. Later that year and early in 1777, General Washington led the Continental Army to a couple of key victories, which boosted morale. In addition, the Continental Congress started to offer cash and land incentives to men to enlist. France became involved, sending weapons, supplies, and eventually troops to help the American revolutionaries. Spain also entered a war against Britain— though not in direct alliance with the Americans, Spanish soldiers battled British troops in Florida. Meanwhile, many American Indians and African slaves fought on the British side. The American Indians were fighting for their own survival, to keep the colonists from moving westward; the slaves believed that a British victory would ensure their freedom.

As the conflict dragged on, it became a war of *attrition* in which the two sides worked to wear each other down. This strategy had adverse effects on both sides—popular support for the war started to flag in Britain, while the American economy suffered and soldiers began to mutiny over not being paid. Then, in 1780 and 1781, revolutionary general Nathanael Greene pushed back the British forces in the Deep South. Finally, in the fall of 1781, American and French forces under the command of General Washington overpowered the British army at Yorktown, Virginia. The consequent surrender of General Cornwallis marked the final major event of the war, though minor battles would continue for the next two years. The official end of the war came in 1783 with the signing of the Treaty of Paris, which recognized the United States as "free sovereign and independent."

While the war was raging, the Second Continental Congress also worked to outline a structure for the government of the new country. They drafted the Articles of Confederation, which would serve as a temporary constitution from 1781 until the current constitution was written in 1787. The most important provision of the Articles of Confederation was the first one: it united all thirteen colonies as "the United States of America." In chapter 4, we will return to the unique system of government that was created over the years following the Revolutionary War.

REAL ESTATE AT ROCK BOTTOM PRICES: THE LOUISIANA PURCHASE

In the early 1800s, France still owned quite a bit of land in North America. In particular, it controlled a large area west of the Mississippi River, which included the city of New Orleans. This region was called Louisiana Territory. New Orleans was an important shipping city for the United States, and in 1801 President Thomas Jefferson sent a delegation to France to offer to buy the city for about $2 million dollars. France, which was led at the time by Napoleon, originally said "no." However, over the next few years, France lost control of some of its island colonies in the Caribbean, and was on the brink of yet another war with Britain. In need of money, Napoleon offered in 1803 to sell all of Louisiana Territory to the United States for a mere $15 million. Jefferson knew it was too good a deal to pass up, and he quickly agreed. The transaction, known as the Louisiana Purchase, effectively doubled the size of the United States, and the area acquired now makes up all or part of fifteen states: Arkansas, Missouri, Iowa, Kansas, North and South Dakota, Oklahoma, New Mexico, Minnesota, Texas, Montana, Nebraska, Wyoming, Louisiana, and Colorado.

THE WAR OF 1812

1799–1803	1805–1810	1807	1812–1813	1814	1815
Beginning of Napoleonic Wars	Various trade restrictions	Chesapeake Affair	War declared / U.S. invades Canada	British defeat Napoleon, attack U.S. / Treaty of Ghent signed	Battle of New Orleans

The War of 1812 was a strange one—neither side really wanted to fight, it did not accomplish anything in terms of territory, and the most famous battle took place after the conflict was officially over!

In the early part of the nineteenth century, Britain was again at war with France, this time trying to quell the advancement of French forces under an ambitious general named Napoleon. As both Britain and France were important trading partners for American goods, the United States did everything it could to remain neutral; however, the warring countries refused to accept U.S. neutrality. The British navy was very powerful, and around 1805, it started seizing American ships that were destined for trade in France. France as well started confiscating commerce ships that had stopped in British ports. In essence, the two countries imposed trade restrictions and naval blockades on each other, and the U.S. was the big loser.

Britain also began raiding American ships looking for British citizens who could be forced into military service—they often took U.S. citizens along as well, a practice which was not looked on favorably in the U.S. This situation came to a head in 1807 when the British navy attacked the *Chesapeake*, an American ship, killing several Americans, in search of four deserters. In addition, the U.S. suspected that Britain was aiding American Indian tribes in regions west of the states' territories, thus preventing the country from expanding into new areas.

Meanwhile, within the U.S. there were two factions—those in favor of a war with

Macdonough's victory on Lake Champlain / painted by H. Reinagle ; engraved by B. Tanner.

Britain and those against it. British trade was the main source of revenue in the northern colonies, and citizens in these areas were not enthusiastic about waging war against their best commerce partner. (In fact, despite the restrictions, the New England states continued relatively unfettered trade with Britain during this time.) In the southern and western parts of the country, however, many saw a war with Britain as a way to conquer additional territory, in particular Canada and Florida (at the time, Florida was a colony of Spain). In 1811, several new members from these southern and western areas were elected to Congress. Known as the "War Hawks," they promoted their ideas, and in June of 1812, the United States declared its first war as an independent nation. (In a bit of dramatic irony, Britain had decided to stop raiding American ships two days prior to Congress's declaration of war—of course, no one in the U.S. knew that at the time!).

During the beginning of the war, Britain was still heavily involved in its conflict with France, and the U.S. decided to take advantage of this fact by invading Canada. American forces were poorly trained and not well equipped, and these advances were quickly rebuffed. In the first major "battle," American forces tried to enter Canada by crossing the Detroit River. However, hearing that there were British, Canadian, and Indian forces waiting on the other side, American Brigadier General William Hull surrendered without even firing a shot. In a second attempt, American forces tried to enter Canada through the Niagara River, but were easily vanquished by British troops—the reinforcements were members of state militias who could not be convinced to cross the border to fight. Another attempt was made, this time to capture certain strongholds in Quebec, but forces marching out of Plattsburgh, New York, made it about twenty miles before turning around and marching right back to Plattsburgh!

By 1814, Britain had won the war with France and had more resources to devote to the war with the U.S., launching attacks in the north, the capital region, and the south. In the north, the two sides faced off in a naval battle on Lake Champlain in which the U.S. eventually prevailed. In retaliation for American troops setting fire to the Canadian capitol in York, British troops stormed Washington, D.C., sending the politicians fleeing. They ate a meal that had been set for President James Madison and promptly set fire to the White House. British troops then tried to conquer Baltimore, but Fort McHenry had been well fortified and the campaign failed. It was during this battle that Francis Scott Key, a young lawyer watching the bombardment from a ship in the harbor, was inspired to write a poem that would later be set to music and become the national anthem of the United States: "The Star-Spangled Banner." In addition to these encounters, American troops in other areas of the country were battling against American Indian forces. In 1814, General Andrew Jackson led a coalition consisting of American troops and Cherokee, Creek, and Choctaw Indians to victory against the Red Stick Creek Indians at Horseshoe Bend, Alabama.

In the meantime, British and American representatives were in Ghent, Belgium, negotiating an end to the war. To start with, both sides had demands—the British wanted a neutral area created for American Indian tribes as well as access to the Mississippi River; the Americans wanted Britain to stop kidnapping U.S. citizens and to pay for the ships it had seized. As the war continued, with both sides able to defend their own land, but neither able to invade the other's territory, the demands were dropped. In December 1814, the Treaty of Ghent was signed, ending the war with no concessions made on either side.

Since no one at that time could even have imagined the convenience of a cell phone, it took about two months for news of the peace treaty to reach the troops in North America. This turned out to be bad news for the British, who in January of 1815 launched their southern attack. Even though the Americans were outnumbered, they were well protected and lying in wait. It took less than half an hour for soldiers under General Jackson to soundly defeat the British invaders in the Battle of New Orleans, which even though it technically took place after the war had ended, became one of the most decisive battles of the conflict. Although the borders remained the same as they had been prior to the war, the United

States had proved that it could defend itself, which led to a sense of identity and unification across the country, even between the northern and southern factions that had disagreed on whether or not to wage the war in the first place.

THE INDIAN WARS

Although the original European settlers often developed cooperative relationships with the American Indians, there were conflicts as well. Many of the first settlers may not have survived in their new environment if it had not been for the help of Native peoples, who showed them how to farm and harvest crops in the new land. Indeed, this cooperation between white and Native Americans forms the basis of the Thanksgiving tradition. As more and more settlers came and the population started to move west, American Indians were pushed into smaller and smaller areas. Sometimes the white settlers would purchase or bargain for Indian territory, but often they just took it by force. Large numbers of American Indians were killed in direct fighting with white settlers, as well as by disease and starvation. On the other hand, many Indians sided with white Americans in some of the wars discussed in this chapter.

The Indian Wars were a series of conflicts that took place from the early 1600s until the late 1890s. The first scrimmages were mainly between individual colonies and individual Indian tribes. As

Sitting Bull (1831?–1890), Native American leader of the Sioux, born in the region of the Grand River in present-day South Dakota. Led by Sitting Bull, the Sioux resisted efforts of the United States government to annex their lands and force them to settle on reservations. Between June 25 and June 26, 1876, the Sioux, with the aid of other tribes, annihilated a punitive expedition commanded by Lieutenant Colonel George Armstrong Custer in the Battle of Little Bighorn.

white settlers started to move west, they met more resistance from Indians who already inhabited the land. At the time, American Indians were often portrayed to the public as barbarians with a thirst for blood and little sense of morality and decency. Of course, this was not true. The settlers themselves and the American or

British armed forces were just as often the aggressors, and were seen by the Indians as invaders of their territory. The settlers also caused the destruction of the buffalo herds upon which many tribes depended, and many American Indians died of starvation.

Although the Declaration of Independence stated that "all men are created equal," it took a long time for American Indians to achieve that promised equality. In the early 1800s, the Supreme Court ruled that although Indians could live on American territory, they could not hold title to it, essentially preventing Indians from having any land of their own. In 1830, President Andrew Jackson passed the Indian Removal Act, which allowed the government to negotiate treaties with Indian tribes living east of the Mississippi—Indians would give up their lands and get other territories to the west, called *reservations*. When many tribes refused, Jackson removed them by force. In the late 1830s, thousands of Cherokee Indians died as they were forcibly removed from their homes in Georgia to Indian Territory, in what is now Oklahoma. This forced relocation became known as the Trail of Tears.

As white settlers moved even farther west, removal treaties often gave way to destructive battles between the invading settlers and Indian tribes who were fighting to preserve their way of life. Two of the best-known conflicts are the Battle of Little Bighorn and the Wounded Knee Massacre. In the Battle of Little Bighorn of 1876, Civil War hero George Custer led an army of about 225 men against the Sioux and Cheyenne Indians led by Sioux chief Sitting Bull in Montana Territory. Custer seriously underestimated the size and strength of the Indian forces, and every one of his men was killed. Shortly after, in 1890, several hundred Sioux Indians were killed by U.S. troops at the Wounded Knee Massacre in South Dakota as they were turning themselves in to be transported to another territory.

One by one, American Indian tribes were systematically defeated, pushed back, and placed under the control of the U.S. federal government. Their lands were taken away, and they were forced to abandon their ways of life. Although they are much less bloody than the battles of 200 years ago, conflicts continue between white Americans and American Indians, and American Indians to this day do not always enjoy equal treatment in American society. In recent years, there have been some signs that these long-standing injustices may finally be set aright. Many tribes in the United States and Canada are now prospering under forms of limited self-government, and treaty rights that were violated have been returned to them. At one point in history, the goal was either to eradicate the Native peoples or to force them to adopt the ways of the white settlers. Today, Indian cultures are recognized as rich and valuable by all Americans and the goal is to preserve, as much as possible, the distinct characters and traditions of these unique societies.

SLAVERY

Slavery was a central issue in the relations between states almost before the United States was founded. Because there were economic differences between the northern states and the southern states, there was also a difference in the need for slaves. The northern part of the country had bigger cities and an economy based on industry, whereas the southern states were primarily agricultural. Landowners in the South depended on slave labor to run their tobacco, cotton, and sugar plantations. Many people in the northern states were opposed to slavery, though not necessarily on moral grounds—a large part of it had to do with representation in government. When representatives from the states got together to write the Constitution, they designed a system in which there are two chambers of Congress, the Senate and the House of Representatives. Whereas each state gets two members in the Senate, the number of delegates to the House of Representatives is based on population. Thus, there was disagreement about whether or not to count slaves as part of the population—the southern states wanted slaves to be counted (even though, of course, they could not vote), and the northern states did not. The Founding Fathers came up with the Three-fifths Compromise, which stated that three-fifths of the slave population would be counted when deciding how to disburse taxes and how many representatives each state would get.

The issue also came up when new states were added to the Union. Non-slave states wanted to make sure that slave states did not end up with disproportionate representation in Congress. This led to a number of laws being passed to equalize the number of free and slave states that were admitted to the Union. For example, in 1820, Congress passed the Missouri Compromise, which specified that slavery could not exist in certain territory above a latitude line that ran roughly through the middle of the country, except for in Missouri, which was granted statehood at the same time as the free state of Maine.

THE MEXICAN–AMERICAN WAR

1819	1821	1836	1844	1846	1848
U.S. acquires Florida from Spain	Mexico gains independence / Moses Austin settles colony in Texas	Texas declares independence from Mexico	James Polk elected president	U.S. declares war on Mexico	Treaty of Guadalupe Hidalgo signed

In 1819, the United States bought Florida from Spain for $5 million and a promise to keep out of Texas. Two years later, however, Mexico (which included the land from Texas to California) declared its independence from Spain and invited Miles Austin to settle 300 American families in Texas. The settlers signed an agreement to abide by Mexican law (which prohibited slavery), learn Spanish, and practice the Roman Catholic religion. For the most part, this agreement was ignored, and by 1834 there were about 20,000 white settlers plus 2,000 black slaves in the region. The previous year, following a military coup, Antonio Lopez de Santa Anna was elected president of Mexico, and he created a new constitution and imposed restrictions on the provinces. The new government was quite unpopular in many regions, including Texas, which declared itself independent in 1836 and petitioned for annexation by the United States. The annexation of Texas was quite controversial, mainly because Texas had ratified a constitution permitting slavery, and Northerners were concerned about the spread of slavery to new territories. In addition, the presidents of the time, Andrew Jackson and Martin Van Buren, did not want to provoke a war with Mexico. However, Congress voted to accept Texas as a slave state in 1845, after which Mexico cut off all diplomatic relations with the U.S.

In 1844, James Polk was elected president on a promise to acquire California from Mexico. He sent a representative to Mexico to try to buy the territory, and when the Mexican government snubbed him, he decided to pick a fight and take the region

MEXICAN–AMERICAN WAR

In 1845 the United States annexed the Republic of Texas, which had recently won its independence from Mexico. Tension between the United States and Mexico mounted following a dispute over the location of the Texas border. This dispute led to the Mexican–American War (1846–1848). At the conclusion of the war, Mexico ceded a large tract of territory that comprises much of what is now the southwestern United States.

by force. Polk sent troops to areas in and around Mexican territory, and in 1846, after Mexican forces attacked an American patrol that had moved onto Mexican land, the U.S. declared war. The war was drastically one-sided—the U.S. did not lose a single battle—and was unpopular particularly in the northeast part of the country, where it was seen as unjust aggression. (One of the politicians who voted against the declaration of war was an Illinois congressman named Abraham Lincoln, who would soon become involved in a war with disastrous consequences.)

Americans in the southern and western states and territories were supportive of the war; they enjoyed the steady stream of military successes and saw it as an opportunity to expand the country. After two years of fighting, which included American troops capturing Mexico City, the war was ended by the signing of the Treaty of Guadalupe Hidalgo. The treaty granted California, Nevada, Utah, Arizona, and parts of New Mexico, Wyoming, and Colorado to the United States in exchange for about $18 million. Although the Mexican–American War was relatively short and came at a low cost to the U.S., it was significant in that the country saw its size increase by about one-fourth with the signing of the peace treaty. The newly acquired territory saw a massive influx of immigrants from around the world after gold was discovered in California in 1848.

MOVIN' ON WEST

After the original thirteen states, the rest of the country grew gradually as a result of settlements, treaties, and in some cases wars. In the mid-1800s, many people believed that the United States was determined by God to extend from the Atlantic Ocean to the Pacific, a principle known as "Manifest Destiny." The principle was used to justify the expansion of American territory westward, even if it meant dishonest dealings or destructive conflicts with the people already living there.

A process was established whereby newly settled or acquired land would become a "territory" administered by the federal government. When its population and development reached a certain level (or perhaps when a valuable resource, such as gold, was discovered), the territory could apply for statehood. By looking at when states were formally admitted to the Union, the expansion of the nation can be charted. As can be seen from the dates listed in the table below, the growth of the country wasn't an orderly movement from east to west. Some areas, such as California, were settled and achieved statehood well before other regions farther east. In 1959, Alaska and Hawaii became the last two states to be admitted into the country.

Delaware	1787	Louisiana	1812	West Virginia	1863
Pennsylvania	1787	Indiana	1816	Nevada	1864
New Jersey	1787	Mississippi	1817	Nebraska	1867
Georgia	1788	Illinois	1818	Colorado	1876
Connecticut	1788	Alabama	1819	North Dakota	1889
Massachusetts	1788	Maine	1820	South Dakota	1889
Maryland	1788	Missouri	1821	Montana	1889
South Carolina	1788	Arkansas	1836	Washington	1889
New Hampshire	1788	Michigan	1837	Idaho	1890
Virginia	1788	Florida	1845	Wyoming	1890
New York	1788	Texas	1845	Utah	1896
North Carolina	1789	Iowa	1846	Oklahoma	1907
Rhode Island	1790	Wisconsin	1848	New Mexico	1912
Vermont	1791	California	1850	Arizona	1912
Kentucky	1792	Minnesota	1858	Alaska	1959
Tennessee	1796	Oregon	1859	Hawaii	1959
Ohio	1803	Kansas	1861		

THE CIVIL WAR

1854	1858	1860	1861	1862	1865
Kansas–Nebraska Act	Lincoln–Douglas debates	Lincoln elected president South Carolina secedes from Union	10 more states secede from Union War begins	Emancipation Proclamation	Lee surrenders to Grant at Appomattox Courthouse Lincoln assassinated

Disagreements over whether to allow slavery in the new territories continued, and in 1854 Congress passed the Kansas–Nebraska Act, which basically repealed the Missouri Compromise of 1820 and stated that settlers in the new territories could decide for themselves whether or not to allow slaves, an idea known as *popular sovereignty*. This sparked a rush to see who could populate the territories first—proslavery or antislavery advocates—as well as debates in government over the power of the states versus the power of the federal government. In 1858, two candidates for an Illinois Senate position, Abraham Lincoln and Stephen Douglas, held a series of debates on the issue. Douglas argued for popular sovereignty. Lincoln, on the other hand, argued that the United States could not survive as a divided country, and that allowing slavery to spread into new territories would essentially allow it into every part of the country, a prospect which he found unacceptable. Lincoln did not, however, argue in favor of freeing all the slaves and giving them the same rights as white people; his primary concern was for the preservation of the United States of America. There were groups of people, called *abolitionists*, mainly in the North, who objected to slavery on moral and religious grounds, but even many Northerners were concerned that if all of the slaves were set free, there would be too much competition for jobs, which would drive down wages.

There were other differences between the North and the South as well, so much so that they almost looked like two different countries. The economy of the

Officers of 3d Pennsylvania Heavy Artillery, Fort Monroe, Virginia.

Northern states was based on industrialization, and was booming at the time. More people in the North lived in cities—by 1860, there were over 800,000 people in New York City and close to 600,000 in Philadelphia. Along with increased production and the building of railroads came higher incomes. The South was still very rural—its largest city, New Orleans, had only about 169,000 people—and its economy depended on exporting cotton, tobacco, and sugar, and importing manufactured products. By and large, this importing and exporting was done by Northern businesses using Northern ships, and many in the South came to feel that they were too financially dependent on the North. In addition, the South had less than half the population and more

than three times the illiteracy rate of the North. As evidenced by the popular sovereignty debate, there were also political differences between the two sections of the country—the North believed in a strong federal government, whereas the South advocated a weaker central government and giving more power to individual states.

Following Lincoln's election as President of the United States in 1860, seven states seceded from the Union: South Carolina, Mississippi, Florida, Alabama, Georgia, Louisiana, and Texas. Representatives from these states gathered to create their own country called the Confederate States of America. They drafted their own constitution and elected Jefferson Davis as their president. Lincoln,

Slaves were commonly bought and sold at slave auctions. Families were often split up as parents and children were sold to different owners. In March of 1859, the largest recorded slave auction in the U.S. took place—436 men, women, and children were sold.

however, did not agree with these states that they had a right to secede; he asserted that it was illegal for states to override the supremacy of the federal government and that the only way for the states to gain independence was through revolution, which is exactly what happened.

As the states seceded, they took control of the federal resources and properties within their borders. At the end of 1860, U.S. forces moved into Fort Sumter in Charleston Bay, South Carolina. South Carolina demanded the withdrawal of the troops, but this request was denied, so the Confederate government sent an army to the area. President Lincoln ordered an unarmed supply ship to be sent to the troops. Upon hearing of Lincoln's plan to restock the fort, Davis ordered his forces to attack. Thus, early in the morning on April 12, 1861, the Confederacy officially fired the first shots of the American Civil War. The battle ended in the surrender of the Union (as the North came to be called) forces.

The attack on Fort Sumter rallied support for the war in both the North and the South. Lincoln called on state militias to provide men, and got more than twice the number that he asked for. In the South, four states—Virginia, Arkansas, Tennessee, and North Carolina—seceded to join the Confederacy. The United States was sharply divided in half, and it was not uncommon for members of the same family to be fighting on opposite sides. Many people, particularly in the North, thought that the war would be over quickly, and no one at that time could imagine that it would be four years and

$200 Reward.

RANAWAY from the subscriber, on the night of Thursday, the 30th of Sepember,

FIVE NEGRO SLAVES,

To-wit: one Negro man, his wife, and three children.

The man is a black negro, full height, very erect, his face a little thin. He is about forty years of age, and calls himself *Washington Reed*, and is known by the name of Washington. He is probably well dressed, possibly takes with him an ivory headed cane, and is of good address. Several of his teeth are gone.

Mary, his wife, is about thirty years of age, a bright mulatto woman, and quite stout and strong.

The oldest of the children is a boy, of the name of FIELDING, twelve years of age, a dark mulatto, with heavy eyelids. He probably wore a new cloth cap.

MATILDA, the second child, is a girl, six years of age, rather a dark mulatto, but a bright and smart looking child.

MALCOLM, the youngest, is a boy, four years old, a lighter mulatto than the last, and about equally as bright. He probably also wore a cloth cap. If examined, he will be found to have a swelling at the navel.

Washington and Mary have lived at or near St. Louis, with the subscriber, for about 15 years.

It is supposed that they are making their way to Chicago, and that a white man accompanies them, that they will travel chiefly at night, and most probably in a covered wagon.

A reward of $150 will be paid for their apprehension, so that I can get them, if taken within one hundred miles of St. Louis, and $200 if taken beyond that, and secured so that I can get them, and other reasonable additional charges, if delivered to the subscriber, or to THOMAS ALLEN, Esq., at St. Louis, Mo. The above negroes, for the last few years, have been in possession of Thomas Allen, Esq., of St. Louis.

WM. RUSSELL.

ST. LOUIS, Oct. 1, 1847.

Slaves who were able to escape were often rounded up and returned to their masters. Sometimes even free black men in the North were kidnapped and sold to Southern slaveowners.

more than 618,000 deaths later that the bloodiest war in American history would finally come to an end.

From one perspective, it looked like the North would win easily—it had more people (about 22 million compared with 9 million in the South), more manufacturing (thus, the army was better supplied), and more railroads; it controlled the navy, and had the help of many European immigrants who came over during the period. What the South lacked in resources, however, it made up for in things less tangible. The South had inherited better military leaders, which gave the Confederacy a decided advantage at the beginning of the conflict. In addition, whereas the Union army had to invade and conquer Southern regions to prevail, the South had only to defend what it already possessed. Members of the Confederate army were fighting, literally, for their homes and their land. The South also had a more concrete ideology to stand behind. Whereas Northerners were fighting for the preservation of the Union (which was still relatively new) and against the expansion of slavery (about which not everyone in the North agreed), Southerners were fighting for the preservation of their way of life.

The North's first plan was to impose a naval blockade on the South, to prevent the South from exporting its crops and importing supplies. In the beginning, this strategy was relatively unsuccessful, but then the South made a grave tactical error. Roughly three-quarters of the cotton shipped by the South went to Britain, and the South reasoned that if it cut off its cotton exports, Britain would come out in support of the Confederate cause. So, the South placed an embargo on cotton exports in 1861. Unfortunately for the South, however, the cotton crops in 1859 and 1860 had been very good and Britain had built up a stockpile, so it did not come to the aid of the South. By the time the embargo was lifted in 1862, the North's naval blockade was much more effective (helped by several Union victories in Southern ports), and the South found it much more difficult to export its crops.

*Portraits of Maj. Gen. Ulysses S. Grant, officer of the Federal Army (left)
and Gen. Robert E. Lee, officer of the Confederate Army (right).*

At the beginning of the war, other than some victories at sea, the Union suffered from poor military leadership and the Confederate army had some significant victories, for example, in the Battle of Bull Run in Virginia. At that time, the North was still expecting a quick and easy victory, and many people came out to watch the battle. Some even brought a picnic lunch! After it became apparent that the war would take longer than expected, the North promoted General Ulysses S. Grant to a position of leadership, which led to a series of wins for the Union army. The South, however, also found new leadership, accomplishing a string of victories under General Robert E. Lee.

In September 1862, Union forces prevented Lee from invading Northern territory at Antietam in Maryland. President Lincoln used this semi-victory as a background on which to issue the Emancipation Proclamation. The proclamation stated that as of January 1, 1863, all slaves in "rebellious" states would be set free. Although the act did not immediately free any slaves, the focus of the war was changed from being a conflict over preserving the Union to also being a fight for liberty. Meanwhile, the North had been successful at holding back invasions by the South, but it had not been able to adequately penetrate into Southern lands. During this time, the South began feeling the effects of the naval blockade and some

District of Columbia. Company E, 4th U.S. Colored Infantry, at Fort Lincoln.

poor economic decisions. Inflation went through the roof, and a food shortage led to discontent among civilians as well as the troops.

During the summer of 1863, the North had several significant victories as General Grant's army prevailed in the Battle of Gettysburg, in Pennsylvania, and the Battle of Vicksburg, in Mississippi, which gave the North control over the Mississippi River and effectively split the South in half. Around this time, the North also started recruiting black men to serve in the army—many slaves had escaped from their masters and crossed into Union territory. It is estimated that more than 125,000 black

men served in Union forces, though they were frequently not combat troops and always served under white leaders.

In 1864, the South realized that it could probably not overpower the North militarily, and it began to wage a war of attrition in the hopes of inflicting enough casualties on Northern forces to weaken their morale. To an extent, this strategy worked. For the first part of the year, there were several battles between armies led by General Lee and General Grant, some of which ended in stalemates, some of which the Confederate army won. The tide turned, however, in September when Union General William Sherman succeeded in taking control of Atlanta, Georgia. After

First reading of the Emancipation Proclamation before the Cabinet.

running off the Confederate forces and ordering the civilian population to evacuate, Sherman's army set about burning the city to the ground. Sherman proceeded to march south from Atlanta to Savannah, and then north through South Carolina and North Carolina, leaving a trail of destruction in his wake.

Finally, in April of 1865, Union forces forced General Lee out of Richmond (the Confederate capital) and Petersburg to Appomattox, Virginia. Upon learning the strength of the Northern army that was waiting for him, Lee had no choice but to surrender to General Grant on April 9. This event marked the symbolic end of the war, and smaller Confederate armies continued to surrender through June of that year.

Relieved at the Union victory as well as at being re-elected, President Lincoln decided to take in a play at Ford's Theater on April 14, 1865. During the show, actor and Southern sympathizer John Wilkes Booth broke into Lincoln's private box and shot the president in the head. Lincoln died the next morning; Booth was cornered and killed a few weeks later. In the end, Lincoln did not live to see the country reunited or the incredible efforts of reconstruction that took place in the years following the war. He certainly solidified his place in history, however, as the president whose struggle freed the slaves and whose vision and dedication saved the United States of America from dissolution.

RECONSTRUCTION

At the end of the Civil War, Americans were faced with the difficult task of putting the country back together again, and much of this struggle played out in the political arena. The two main political parties in the United States were the Republican Party and the Democratic Party, though at the time they were quite different from the parties that bear those names now. The  Democratic Party had emerged in the late eighteenth century and drew much of its support from the South; thus, Democrats tended to be those who were in favor of slavery and had supported the Confederacy. The Republican Party, however, was brand new. It was started in 1854 and its founders were opposed to slavery. It got most of its backing from the North.

Although Lincoln had been a member of the Republican Party, his vice president, Andrew Johnson, who assumed the presidency after Lincoln's assassination, was a southern Democrat. Since Congress at the time was dominated by Republicans, there was a considerable amount of disagreement over how to reintegrate the southern states into the Union and what to do with the almost 4 million slaves who had been freed and who were living, by and large, in the South. In addition, the South had been severely ravaged by the war—there was little business and little money, and with the end of slavery came the end of the plantation, which had been the mainstay of the South's economy. (In December 1865, the Thirteenth Amendment to the Constitution was ratified, officially declaring slavery illegal.)

Many Republicans wanted to take a hard line against Southerners who had rebelled and to give equal voting rights to former slaves. Following a plan that Lincoln had outlined before his death, Southern states were initially to be allowed to rejoin the Union and set up state governments upon a certain percentage of the population swearing an oath of allegiance to the Union. Several states, however, elected Democrats to office who had served as leaders of the Confederacy and passed measures known as "Black Codes," which restricted the rights and liberties of blacks.

The Republicans saw these measures as just a new version of slavery, and Union forces were required to stop their implementation in several areas.

President Johnson as well seemed to favor policies that restored the previous imbalance of power between the races. Under his policies, much of the Southern land that had been confiscated by Union forces was simply returned to the previous owners. Most ex-slaves could not buy land, either because it was too expensive or because white owners refused to sell, and many had little choice but to return to the plantations to work for low wages or for a share of the crops produced. As has happened many times in the history of many countries, high levels of unemployment led to increased crime, and vigilante groups (who were usually made up of white supremacists) began to spring up in many parts of the South. For example, in 1865 an organization known as the Ku Klux Klan was established for the purpose of controlling the black population through intimidation and violence.

In 1866, Congress passed the Fourteenth Amendment stating that all people born or naturalized in the U.S. were American citizens, and in 1867, it passed the Reconstruction Acts. These laws divided the southern states into five military districts and gave voting rights to all males twenty-one years of age and older. The acts also specified that the states were required to ratify the Fourteenth Amendment before their elected representatives would be recognized in Congress. Southern Democrats were not happy with this arrangement; neither was President Johnson, but he was replaced by Ulysses S. Grant the following year.

By 1870, all of the southern states had rejoined the Union, and the Fifteenth Amendment, which specified that the right to vote could not be denied on the basis of "race, color or previous condition of servitude," had been ratified. In fact, between 1868 and 1874, sixteen black men were elected to Congress.

Unfortunately for the civil rights movement of the time, the presidency of Ulysses S. Grant was plagued by corruption—not the man himself, but many of his aides and advisors were deeply involved in swindling money from taxpayers. One of the consequences of this was that in the congressional election of 1874, Democrats gained control of many new seats in government. By that time, many in the North (the politicians as well as the citizens) were tired of the "Southern Question," and were ready to just leave the South alone to do as it pleased. In 1876, Republican Rutherford B. Hayes ran for president against Democrat Samuel J. Tilden. Throughout the South, the Democratic Party used violence and intimidation to keep black voters away from the polls. The results of the election were close enough that a special electoral commission was appointed to decide who had won. Finally, in 1877, the Democrats agreed to recognize Hayes as president in return for the withdrawal of federal troops from the South, thus marking the end of the Reconstruction Era. Although in theory black and white men had equal rights and blacks were allowed to vote, in practice the Democratic governments set up in many states spent the next several years passing measures that prevented blacks from achieving that equality. It would be almost a century before many blacks would be able to take full advantage of the rights guaranteed them under the Constitution. In addition, white resentment toward blacks for their role in toppling the Southern way of life would lead to an entrenchment of racial prejudice that in many ways is still evident today.

Theodore Roosevelt and his "Rough Riders" became heroes for their exploits in the Battle of San Juan Hill.

THE SPANISH–AMERICAN WAR

1800s	January	February	April	Summer/Fall	December
Cubans rebel against Spain	U.S. consul in Cuba requests warship	Maine explodes in Havana Harbor	U.S. declares war on Spain	U.S. defeats Spain in Cuba, Puerto Rico, the Philippines	Peace treaty signed

1898

In 1898, the United States entered into a war that was relatively short and painless (certainly compared to the Civil War!). The causes of the war were questionable, but in the end, only a few hundred Americans had been killed or injured, and the U.S. had established itself as a military power that could compete on a global scale.

Since Christopher Columbus landed in Cuba in the late 1400s, the island had belonged to Spain. During the 1800s, Cubans rebelled against colonial rule, and by the end of the century rebel troops controlled much of the island. To regain control, Spain sent troops under the command of a general who became known as "The Butcher" for his brutality toward the Cuban people. The Butcher forced hundreds of thousands of Cubans into concentration camps, where many of them died of starvation and disease. Perhaps because they had so recently won their own independence, and because the U.S. was one of Cuba's best clients for sugar cane, Americans sympathized with the Cubans. In addition, the main newspapers in the U.S. at the time were all trying to "out-sensationalize" each other to increase their sales, and their reports of Spain's viciousness toward the Cubans were greatly exaggerated. The newspapers also published a letter written by a Spanish

The Spanish–American war was fought in the Spanish colonies of the Philippines and Cuba. On June 22, 1898, the United States landed 15,000 soldiers southeast of Santiago de Cuba. The troops engaged and defeated Spanish land forces on July 1st.

minister in which he accused President McKinley of being "weak," which did not do much to improve Spanish–American relations.

In January 1898, because of considerable disorder in the Cuban capital of Havana, the U.S. consul to Cuba asked for a warship to be sent to protect American citizens and property. The U.S. responded by sending the *Maine* to Havana Harbor. On February 15, the ship exploded and sank. At the time, a U.S. report concluded that the explosion had been caused by a

mine, whereas a Spanish report concluded that it had been because of internal problems. (A recent study suggested that it may have been the result of spontaneous combustion in the coal bunkers.) In any case, many Americans were more than happy to place the blame squarely on Spain, and on April 11, McKinley asked Congress to authorize a war. Spain had actually declared an armistice a couple of days earlier, but McKinley was not overly concerned with that small detail, and by the end of the month, the two countries were at war.

In spite of his initial reluctance, President William McKinley could not avoid bowing to political pressure. On April 11, 1898, he asked Congress for a declaration of war against Spain.

John Hay, the U.S. ambassador to Great Britain at the time, called the conflict "a splendid little war," and from the American perspective, it was. Although the U.S. army was not equal to Spanish forces, the navy was superior, and the first thing the U.S. did was to impose a naval blockade on the island. Naval victories, together with a few successes on land, led to the U.S. gaining control of Cuba by mid-July and of Puerto Rico by the end of the month. Two months later, the U.S. navy again overpowered Spanish forces, this time in the Philippines, and on December 10, the two countries signed a peace treaty ending the war. According to the terms of the treaty, Spain withdrew from Cuba and ceded Puerto Rico, Guam, and the Philippines to the U.S. in exchange for about $20 million. To this day, Puerto Rico and Guam remain territories of the U.S.; the Philippines gained independence in 1946.

The war accomplished two things: first, it established the U.S. as a global military power, and second, it catapulted former Assistant Secretary of the Navy Theodore Roosevelt to instant fame. Roosevelt led a voluntary cavalry called the "Rough Riders," made up of ranchers, businessmen, polo players, and a few ex-convicts. The troops were sent to Cuba in June, though because of transportation problems, they arrived without their horses. Roosevelt's Rough Riders participated in a few of the major battles on Cuban soil, and though they were outnumbered, they showed considerable bravery, soundly defeating the Spanish. Roosevelt went on to serve two terms as the President of the United States.

THE AMERICAN–FILIPINO WAR

Perhaps because it is not a particularly bright spot in American military history, the American–Filipino War is often overlooked. According to the peace treaty signed with Spain at the end of the Spanish–American War, the United States acquired the Philippines. This led to disagreements at home between Americans who thought the country should be imperialist, or strive to extend its rule to other nations, and those who did not. In addition, the agreement aroused much discontent in the Filipinos, who wanted their independence. For about four years, American soldiers fought Filipino insurgents, and their vicious tactics were not all that different from those that they had just condemned on the part of Spain in Cuba. In the end, a combined policy of accommodating Filipinos who submitted to American rule and harshly punishing those who did not brought the revolt to its conclusion.

WORLD WAR I

1914	1915	1917	1918	1919
Austro-Hungarian archduke assassinated War begins	*Lusitania* sunk by German U-boat submarine	U.S. declares war on Germany Russia negotiates armistice with Germany	Allied troops stave off German offensive on western front Germany asks for armistice	Treaty of Versailles signed

U.S. 7th Machine Gun Battalion, 3rd Division at Chateau Thierry bridgehead.

World War I began in 1914 when Austro-Hungarian archduke and heir to the throne Franz Ferdinand was assassinated by a Bosnian nationalist in a protest for Bosnia's independence. At first, it looked as if this matter could be confined to Eastern Europe; however, because of military alliances between European countries that basically stated, "If you attack one of us, you attack all of us," Germany, Austria-Hungary, and the Ottoman Empire (the Central Powers) were quickly pitted against Britain, France, and the Russian Empire (the Allied Powers, or Allies). Throughout the course of the war, many more countries would become involved.

The United States, under President Woodrow Wilson, announced an official policy of neutrality—this was a European war that had nothing to do with America—but as time passed, the U.S. became less and less neutral. In proclaiming its neutrality, the U.S. planned to continue commerce with countries on both sides of the conflict. However, Britain and France roughly quadrupled their demand for American food and supplies, and a British naval blockade all but cut off trade between the U.S. and Germany. U.S. banks also loaned large sums of money to the Allies in order to finance their war effort. Thus, in addition to sharing a language and a cultural background with Britain, during

the first part of the war, the booming U.S. economy depended heavily on the Allies.

World War I was a "modern" war—new technologies brought with them new, more efficient means of warfare. For Germany, this came in the form of a submarine, called a U-boat. Submarines could carry out devastating attacks on other ships with relatively little warning, and on May 7, 1915, a German U-boat sank a British passenger ship, the *Lusitania*, killing about 1,350 people including 128 Americans. The circumstances surrounding the sinking of the *Lusitania* were suspicious from the start. Germany had warned that it would sink any ship in British waters that was carrying munitions, and the German embassy had posted a warning next to advertisements

for the *Lusitania* that a war was being conducted in the area where the ship was scheduled to sail. Although the *Lusitania* was a passenger ship, it was also secretly carrying munitions headed for British ports. In the days prior to the arrival of the *Lusitania* in British waters, at least two other ships were sunk by U-boats. Still, Americans were shocked at what they saw as an unprovoked German attack on civilians. Despite this incident, President Wilson still managed to keep the U.S. out of the war, at least for a little while longer.

In early 1917, two events coincided to propel the U.S. into the war. First, in February, it was revealed that Germany had attempted to make a military alliance with Mexico, in the case that the United States declared war against Germany. In return for attacking the U.S., Germany promised to return to Mexico the territories that it had ceded in the Mexican–American War. Second, in March, the czar of the Russian Empire was overthrown and a fragile liberal democratic government put in place. Thus, when President Wilson asked Congress in April for authorization to declare war on Germany, he gave as a reason that "the world must be made safe for democracy."

There was much opposition in the U.S. to the country's involvement in the war, so the federal government launched a huge public relations campaign. Wilson established the Committee on Public

EUROPE
Before and After World War I

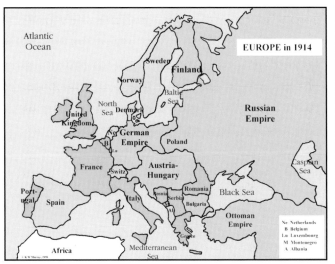

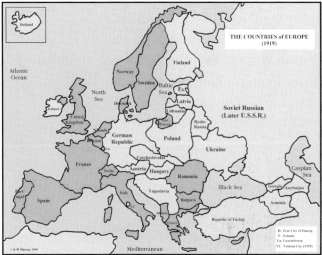

Information (CPI) to distribute pro-war propaganda in the form of speeches, films, posters, and advertisements. The CPI recruited celebrities to tout the pro-war message and to promote the sale of war bonds to finance the effort. These actions led to a lot of anti-German sentiment in the United States, and were followed by the passage of a series of laws that severely restricted the freedom of speech guaranteed to all Americans by the First Amendment to the Constitution.

The war (known as the Great War) also gave rise to a practice that became very controversial in future military conflicts: the draft. A draft allows the government to call for mandatory military service at times when the volunteer forces are not

sufficient. A draft had been in use during the Civil War, but under that system, a person could pay someone else to take his place. This led to disproportionate casualties among the lower classes. According to the Selective Service Act of 1917, replacement soldiers were no longer allowed, and according to current law, every male U.S. citizen is required to register for the draft upon turning eighteen.

American involvement in the war came none too soon for the beleaguered French and British armies. In late 1917, after a second revolution, Russia negotiated an armistice with Germany, following which Germany focused much of its efforts on the western front. In early 1918, German forces invaded France and came very close to taking control of Paris. American troops arrived just in time to help the French military repel the German attackers, and succeeded in pushing them back to the German border. After more than 40 million people had been killed or wounded worldwide, Germany asked for an armistice on November 11, 1918. The Treaty of Versailles, which officially ended the war, was signed in June of 1919. The treaty was highly punitive against Germany: it placed legal and military restrictions on Germany, forced the country to cede the colonies it had conquered, and required Germany to pay extremely high reparations for having caused the war. The peace that was achieved would not endure, and just about twenty years later, the world would be thrown into an even bigger conflict.

Woodrow Wilson's firm belief that the seas should be kept safe from German U-boats, coupled with growing pro-British sentiments in the United States, led to America entering World War I on April 6, 1917.

THE ROARING '20s AND THE DEPRESSED '30s

In the years after the Great War, Americans were in the mood to kick up their heels and forget their troubles for awhile—they had shorter workdays and workweeks, and the economy was still thriving from the boost it got during the war, so many people also had more money to spend. The 1920s saw the development of mass media leading to an explosion of a uniquely American culture. People with extra time and money on their hands went to movies (the first full-length "talking picture" was released in 1927), listened to the radio, and played games and sports. Jazz established itself as the quintessential American form of music. The idea of celebrity also caught on, as people began to idolize the likes of Babe Ruth and Charles Lindbergh. The decade brought a shift in relations between the sexes—during the war, many women had gone to work outside of the home for the first time. In addition, women got the right to vote in 1920, which contributed to their growing sense of independence. Finally (and not to everyone's advantage), the "Roaring '20s" saw the development of a new economic system in the country. Consumer credit was introduced, leading to the purchasing of goods on installment plans. For many people, the money they were spending on entertainment and popular culture was not necessarily money they could afford to spend.

In October of 1929, the fun, carefree lifestyle that characterized the '20s came to an end when the stock market crashed sending the country into a prolonged period of economic hardship known as the Great Depression. There were many reasons why the depression occurred, which can be boiled down to the fact that the economy had been growing too much too quickly, and the bubble finally burst. The Great Depression was felt worldwide, and it resulted in soaring unemployment rates and a reduction in manufacturing. In 1932, Franklin D. Roosevelt was elected President of the United States, and shortly after he introduced a series of programs called the New Deal to help the country out of its slump. Among other things, the New Deal created jobs by instituting civic works projects such as building roads and schools, provided for banking reform, and helped farmers who had seen demand for their products decrease. Roosevelt also passed the Social Security Act providing retirement pensions and unemployment insurance, and set a minimum wage and maximum workweek for American laborers. It took almost a decade, but by 1940, things were looking up.

WORLD WAR II

1931	1933	1938	1939	1940	1941	1944			
Japan invades China	Hitler's Nazi Party elected in Germany	Germany invades Austria	Germany invades Poland / Britain, France declare war on Germany	German *blitzkrieg* / Italy declares war on Britain and France	Japan attacks Pearl Harbor / U.S. declares war on Japan	D-Day invasions	Hitler commits suicide / Germany surrenders	U.S. drops atomic bombs on Hiroshima, Nagasaki	Japan surrenders

1945

While the United States was working to pull itself out of the Great Depression, tensions were nearing the boiling point in the rest of the world. In 1931, Japan invaded a portion of China and set up a government. Since the U.S. and other countries were worrying more about domestic problems than foreign ones, the world reaction amounted to little more than a few harsh words. The real trouble started in 1933 when Adolf Hitler's Nazi Party came to power in Germany. The punishments and sanctions placed on Germany at the end of World War I devastated and humiliated the German people, which greatly contributed to their willingness to support the Nazi party. Hitler denounced the Treaty of Versailles and set forth highly nationalistic and racist policies aimed at re-establishing

Germany as a world power. In 1935 Italy entered Ethiopia, and in 1938 Germany invaded Austria; again other countries responded with condemnation of the acts, but little else. In 1939, however, Germany invaded Poland. Poland had been a divided country until the end of World War I, when it regained its independence. Britain and France had pledged to defend Poland in the case that it was attacked, so when the German army entered the country, Britain and France declared war on Germany, officially beginning the Second World War.

The United States again tried to remain neutral and worked to avoid repeating the mistakes it had made prior to World War I— in the mid-1930s, Congress passed neutrality acts placing trade embargos on the countries involved in the conflicts, prohibiting U.S.

The Big Three—Stalin, Roosevelt, and Churchill—during a peace conference in 1943.

institutions from lending money to them, and restricting Americans from traveling on their ships. In 1940, however, Germany launched a *blitzkrieg*, or "lightning war," and the German army quickly marched through and occupied Denmark, the Netherlands, Norway, Belgium, Luxembourg, and France. By this time, Germany, Italy, and Japan had united together as the Axis powers, and the U.S. had started providing support and supplies to Britain.

All hopes for neutrality vanished on December 7, 1941, when Japan launched a surprise attack on the U.S. naval base at Pearl Harbor in Hawaii. The attack left about 2,400 Americans dead and more wounded, and shortly thereafter President Franklin D. Roosevelt asked Congress for authorization to declare war on Japan.

Over the next few years, war would take place both in Europe (against Germany and Italy) and in the Pacific (against Japan), and the Allied powers would grow to include many countries such as Canada, Norway, Greece, India, Yugoslavia, and eventually the Soviet Union.

After Germany's initial advance through Europe, the Allied powers started on the offensive. In 1942, the Allies started bombing targets in Germany and attacked German forces in Africa. In addition, the Soviet Union began pushing Germany back out of Soviet territory that it had invaded earlier in the conflict. On June 6, 1944, known as D-Day, Allied troops launched a massive operation starting on the Normandy coast of France. They eventually succeeded in liberating France

Dwight D. Eisenhower giving orders to American paratroopers in England.

and pushing German troops back to the border. The winter of that year, Germany went on the offensive in a counterattack, but this effort was quickly suppressed by the Allied forces. In April of 1945, Hitler committed suicide, and the next month Germany officially surrendered.

The war in the Pacific followed roughly the same timeline. After its attack on Pearl Harbor, Japan acted quickly to take control of Guam, Hong Kong, Burma, the Philippines, and many other islands in the region. In 1942, the Allies started pushing Japan back. World War II brought an unprecedented boost in military technology, which in turn brought an unprecedented level of destruction and loss of life. In 1945, the U.S. started bombing Japan with napalm, setting fire to large sections of the Japanese landscape.

Later that year, the atrocities of war reached their highest point with the introduction of the atomic bomb into modern warfare.

A group of scientists who had left Germany, including Albert Einstein, warned President Roosevelt that Germany was working to create an atomic bomb, a new and highly effective weapon of mass destruction. The U.S. launched a top secret operation, called the Manhattan Project, to develop the bomb first. In mid-July 1945, the first atomic bomb was detonated at a testing center in New Mexico. Later that month, the Allies demanded that Japan surrender unconditionally, and when Japan refused, President Harry Truman ordered U.S. planes to drop atomic bombs on the cities of Hiroshima and Nagasaki. The destruction was greater than anyone could have imagined. Several hundreds of thousands of people (mostly civilians) were killed by the bombs themselves as well as by the aftereffects of radiation, and the cities were utterly destroyed. Japan surrendered on August 15, 1945.

The casualties of World War II are estimated at about 55 million worldwide. In addition to the military and civilian casualties as a direct result of warfare, many people were killed because of the Nazi regime's racist policies. Hitler had proclaimed that Germans were members of a "master race," and he blamed many of Germany's problems on people of Jewish descent. During the war, the Nazis rounded up millions of Jews and forced them into concentration camps, and ultimately more than 6 million were killed. In addition to Jews, the Nazis exterminated large populations of homosexuals, Jehovah's witnesses, Gypsies, people who were mentally or physically disabled, and pretty much anyone who dared to voice disagreement with Nazi policies. In the United States, even though most people were horrified by the racism of the Nazis, there was a significant amount of animosity directed toward Japanese people after Japan's attack on Pearl Harbor drew the U.S. into the war. In 1942, President Roosevelt signed an order calling for Japanese people to be confined into what were known as *internment camps*, using military necessity as justification for the action. Overall, about 120,000 Japanese people were placed in the camps, more than 60% of whom were American citizens. It wasn't until the 1980s that the U.S. government recognized that the internments were based on racism rather than military necessity, and the U.S. issued a formal apology for the matter.

At home, the war had a great impact on the economy and social relations. War is generally good for a country economically, and during World War II, production was increased and there was a birth of new industry. As so many American men were called to serve in the military, women entered the workforce in even greater numbers. Because of the increase in production, more African Americans moved from farming communities in the south to factory jobs in big cities. President Roosevelt even struck a deal with the Mexican government to allow Mexican workers (some of whom had been kicked out of the country during the '20s and '30s) to enter the U.S. to boost up the workforce. Despite the participation of these and other minority groups in society and in the war effort, the U.S. was still far from being a country where all races were recognized as equal.

One very positive result of World War II was the creation of the United Nations, an international organization aimed at preventing wars and solving disputes between nations, as well as providing humanitarian assistance to people in need. The United Nations works to maintain international peace and security, and to promote international economic and social development and cooperation.

THE KOREAN WAR

1905–1945	1945	1947	1949	1950	1951	1953
Korea occupied by Japan	WWII ends Korea split into North and South Beginning of Cold War	U.S. aid to Greece, Turkey	Communist Party gains power in China	North Korea invades South Korea U.S., U.N. send troops	Stalemate	Armistice agreement signed

SETTING THE STAGE: THE COLD WAR

In 1917, a political party based on the idea of communism gained control in the Russian Empire, which then became known as the Soviet Union. Communism is an economic and political system based on the ideas that the government is heavily involved in pretty much all aspects of life, and that all citizens are essentially equal. For example, there is no private ownership of land and no distinction between economic classes; rather, each person does the work that they are best suited for, and the government provides all the necessities of life. In a communist system, there is neither private ownership nor economic freedom of individuals. In practice, communism is usually equated with a totalitarian government where all the power is in the hands of one or a few people and the citizens are poor and often stripped of their civil liberties. In other words, it is completely the opposite of the democratic, capitalist system that makes up the foundation of the United States.

Following World War II, the Communist Party in the Soviet Union was very strong and was seeking to expand its influence to other parts of the world. The U.S. saw this as a significant threat, and for about forty-five years after the Second World War, the

United States and the Soviet Union were engaged in what was called a *cold war*—a military, economic, political, and cultural rivalry. One of the manifestations of the Cold War was a nuclear arms race in which the countries competed to build more and bigger weapons than each other. The two countries never entered into direct military conflict, but this rivalry played out in many smaller countries worldwide. President Harry Truman adopted a policy of *containment* by which the U.S. would act to stop the spread of communism. For example, in 1947, the U.S. provided financial aid to forces that were trying to quash a communist revolution in Greece and Turkey. Americans were worried about a domino effect—the idea that if one country fell to communism, many more countries would follow suit. Since communism was so different from anything they had ever experienced, many people perceived it as a direct threat to the American way of life.

The popular General Douglas MacArthur served the nation in World War I as a major (and later brigadier general), in World War II as commander of the army in the Far East, and in the Korean War as head of the United Nations military forces.

Between 1905 and 1945, Korea was occupied by Japan. After World War II, Korea was split into two sections—the Soviet Union supported North Korea, and the United States supported South Korea. In 1950, North Korea invaded South Korea in an attempt to reunite the country under a communist regime. The United States convinced the United Nations to send "peacekeeping" forces to conduct a "police action" to help the South Koreans. Later that year U.N. troops (made up primarily of U.S. servicemen) landed in South Korea under the command of General Douglas MacArthur, an American World War II hero.

At first, the campaign was so successful that it appeared the conflict would end immediately—South Korean and U.N. troops were able to push the North Koreans back almost to China,

Korea's neighbor to the north. Unfortunately for the interests of the United States, the Communist Party had gained control of China in 1949. Facing a threat along its border, China sent forces to support North Korea, pushing the U.N. forces almost to the southern tip of the country. Due to the brilliant leadership of General MacArthur, the U.N. troops were able to rally and force the invading North Korean army back to North Korea. Starting in 1951, the war was basically a stalemate. Peace negotiations were ongoing and the bombing continued, but relatively little territory changed hands. In 1953, after a difficult and bloody guerilla war, the two sides agreed to call it a draw and the country remained divided, roughly in the same place it was before.

As the war dragged on and more than 50,000 American soldiers lost their lives, many Americans back home became frustrated, particularly since the war came so closely on the heels of World War II. Many people became paranoid about communism and feared that communist sympathizers at home were partly responsible for the inability of the United States to have a decisive victory abroad. America paid a price for the conflict in Korea, in dollars and lives as well as in division and disagreement about whether or not it was proper for the United States to act as a "policeman" for the world. This issue would come up again and again. The dreaded communism was still a force to be reckoned with, and a few years later the United States would enter a similar conflict in which victory was impossible and which would have a significant long-term impact on the psyche of the country as a whole.

President Harry Truman

THE VIETNAM WAR

1946	1954	1964	1965	1968	1969	1973	1975
Beginning of French Indochina War	France driven out of Vietnam by communist forces / Vietnam split into North and South	Gulf of Tonkin incident / Congress authorizes military action	U.S.-supported regime in South Vietnam falls	Tet offensive	U.S. launches attacks on Laos, Cambodia	U.S., North Vietnam sign peace accord / U.S. withdraws troops	North Vietnam conquers South Vietnam / Vietnam reunited as communist state

Prior to World War II, Vietnam was a French colony (along with Cambodia and Laos), and during the war it was occupied by Japan. Following the war, France reclaimed the colony, but in 1946 an uprising led by communist Ho Chi Minh rebelled against French rule, starting the French Indochina War. During the struggle, the U.S. sent aid to support the French against the communists; however, in 1954 the rebels succeeded— France was driven out of the country. Vietnam was divided in half: North Vietnam had a communist government, and South Vietnam had a democratic government. Over the next few years, in keeping with the policy of containment, the U.S. sent money, advisors, and eventually troops to South Vietnam to prevent the country from being conquered by the Communist North.

In August 1964, an incident took place that changed the course of the conflict. A U.S. Navy ship in the Tonkin Gulf traded fire with North Vietnamese patrol boats. Two days later, the American ship returned to the Gulf and reported another attack by North Vietnam. President Lyndon B. Johnson used this event as a reason to strike North Vietnam directly, and Congress authorized "all necessary measures" to prevent "communist aggression." Shortly thereafter U.S. warplanes started bombing North Vietnamese targets. The ironic thing is that further study has suggested that the second attack on the U.S. Navy ship never happened; recent evidence has also shown that Johnson probably knew that at the time.

In 1965, the U.S.-supported regime in South Vietnam fell. By March of that year, 100,000 American soldiers had been sent to Vietnam; that number would climb to more than 500,000 over the next three years. Early reports suggested that the U.S. was effectively pushing back the North Vietnamese, and most people believed that the war would end in a quick win for the United States. In January of 1968, however, North Vietnamese forces launched a huge campaign, known as the Tet offensive, which caught American forces off guard. Although the communist troops suffered huge casualties, the success of the Tet offensive led many to realize that the U.S. was not in for a quick and easy victory.

In 1968, Richard Nixon was elected President of the United States. For the next few years, he promised to end U.S. involvement in Vietnam while at the same time escalating and expanding the conflict. In 1969, Nixon authorized the bombing of Laos and Cambodia, which had also been part of French Indochina, and the next year he ordered the invasion of Cambodia. Meanwhile, public support for the war in the United States was flagging, and most Americans wanted to see the troops come home. The trouble was, however, that South Vietnam was not capable of fighting its own war. Nixon recognized that it was a lose-lose situation—a withdrawal of U.S. troops would lead to the country being reunited as a communist state. In the end, that is

exactly what happened: in 1973 the U.S. and North Vietnam signed a peace accord providing for the withdrawal of American troops, and in 1975 South Vietnam fell to the Communist North.

The Vietnam War was perhaps the most difficult conflict the United States has ever been involved in. To begin with, the objectives of the war were never made entirely clear, and a lot of the decision making was kept secret. Soldiers on the battlefield as well as Americans at home were not exactly sure what they were fighting for. As the war continued and more and more Americans lost their lives, this lack of real justification had a greater impact. There were mass antiwar demonstrations across the country, and many men fled to Canada or joined the National Guard to avoid being drafted and sent to Vietnam.

The war was also incredibly difficult for the soldiers on the ground. The jungle terrain was unfamiliar and unlike anywhere most of them had ever been. American troops also did not have experience with the types of guerilla tactics that were used in the war. The North Vietnamese recruited young boys to fight, and would even use small children to carry live grenades to U.S. positions. Civilians, including women and children, would be strapped with bombs or used to lure American troops into the bushes. In addition, it was not always easy to tell the allies from the enemies. There was a large resistance movement within South

Television played a critical role in forming popular opinion as disturbing images of death and destruction were broadcast on the evening news (left). Lyndon Johnson's escalation of America's involvement in the conflict was not well received, particularly among younger voters (right).

Vietnam that was taking orders from Communist North Vietnam, and often these resistance fighters would be living in villages otherwise full of allies. In one particularly gruesome incident, the My Lai Massacre, as many as 500 civilians were executed by American troops in a community that was thought to be a resistance stronghold. In the end, it turned out to be a big mistake: only women, children, and elderly men were killed.

Finally, the Vietnam War provoked a large amount of anger and discontent in the American public. War reports were broadcast nightly on news channels, and Americans were exposed for the first time to the real horrors of war. The reports on the news did not always coincide with what the people were hearing from their government. Statistics about American and enemy casualties were announced like baseball scores. There were harrowing scenes of civilians being summarily executed by South Vietnamese police officers and naked villagers running screaming from their destroyed homes, their bodies covered in napalm burns and shrapnel wounds. Americans saw soldiers being loaded onto stretchers, bloody, with parts of limbs blown off by mines, booby traps, or enemy fire. Antiwar sentiment sometimes even led to violent and fatal incidents in the United States, and the feeling of most Americans was that the war just needed to end. By the time the U.S. withdrew its troops, more than 58,000 Americans had been killed and more than 150,000 wounded. More than $150 billion had been spent, and nothing had been gained.

The whole affair would be a bitter pill for the American public to swallow, and would radically effect the willingness to engage in future military conflicts on foreign soil. The reluctance to engage in the type of lengthy, full-scale war effort fought in Vietnam has been dubbed the *Vietnam syndrome.*

THE PERSIAN GULF WAR

In the first part of the 1900s, oil was discovered in the Middle East. Oil consumption quickly went through the roof, and today, the United States gets more than half of its oil from other countries. As the world became more and more dependent on oil, the issue of power in the Middle East became a significant one, and in the 1970s a powerful dictator named Saddam Hussein gained control in Iraq.

For various reasons, tensions had been building between Iraq and neighboring Kuwait, and on August 2, 1990, Iraq invaded and annexed the oil-rich country. George H.W. Bush, who was president at the time, was cautious initially because the United States had previously supported Iraq in a conflict with Iran. However, the U.S. and other countries could not sit back and watch Kuwait's oil be taken by force, and U.S. intelligence suggested that Hussein also had his eye on Saudi Arabia, so Bush took the case to the United Nations. The U.N. denounced Iraq's aggression and authorized the U.S. to use force to free Kuwait if Iraq refused to withdraw. Several world leaders imposed economic sanctions on Iraq, refusing to trade with the country until it left Kuwait.

Hussein refused to pull his troops out, and in January 1991 the United States and allies including Britain, France, and Saudi Arabia launched a massive aerial assault on Iraq. About six weeks later, ground troops entered the conflict and carried out a devastating operation that lasted about four days before Hussein agreed to withdraw his troops. As part of the agreement, Hussein also promised to get rid of Iraq's nuclear and biological weapons capabilities. Kuwait was freed, but the U.S. operation stopped short of relieving Hussein from power, a decision which would come back to haunt the country roughly a decade later.

Many Americans were unsure what to think of the war. On one hand, it had been a staggering success—the U.S. forces were much better equipped than the Iraqi army, and the use of large-scale airstrikes kept American soldiers relatively out of harm's way. In fact, there were fewer than 150 deaths out of the approximately 600,000 Americans who served in the conflict. On the other hand, many people saw the war as being waged solely to protect U.S. oil interests and did not support putting U.S. soldiers in danger for purely economic reasons.

There was another source of controversy surrounding the Gulf War. Although few soldiers actually died in the conflict, many troops returning from the war became ill months or even years later. The causes of these illnesses remain controversial, but recent studies have suggested that they can be attributed to exposure to toxic chemicals. Some of these servicemen and women claimed to have been exposed to chemical or biological warfare agents, and many felt that they did not receive adequate protection or information from the government.

SEPTEMBER 11, 2001

After a highly contested election in 2000, George W. Bush (son of the former president) became President of the United States. On September 11, less than a year into his first term, a massive terrorist attack was carried out on American soil, as militant Islamists loyal to Osama bin Laden's al-Qaeda network hijacked four passenger airliners. Two of the planes crashed into and destroyed the World Trade Center in New York City, the third hit the Pentagon in Washington, D.C., and the fourth was downed in a field in Pennsylvania. In all, the attacks caused the deaths of nearly 3,000 people. President Bush responded by declaring what he called a "War on Terrorism," which would see American troops fighting for many years in Afghanistan and Iraq, and would greatly impact the political landscape of the United States for years to come.

THE WAR IN AFGHANISTAN

September	October	December	2003–2005	2006	2009
9/11 attacks	U.S., Britain launch initial attacks	Taliban removed from power / U.N. sends security forces	Taliban reorganizes, gains strength	International forces start replacing U.S. forces	U.S. sends more troops to Afghanistan

2001

The blame for masterminding the 9/11 attacks was placed squarely on the shoulders of Osama bin Laden, a Saudi Arabian man who founded the terrorist network al-Qaeda. Prior to the attacks, bin Laden had been living in Afghanistan, running terrorist training camps in an alliance with the Taliban, which had been governing the country since 1996.

On October 7, 2001, the United States and Britain launched an attack (mainly airstrikes) against Afghanistan with the stated objectives of capturing bin Laden, destroying the al-Qaeda network, and removing the Taliban from power. Although by and large the American public supported the operation, it was controversial for many reasons. First, there was some evidence that the Bush administration had been planning just

such an attack on Afghanistan before 9/11, calling the motives for the war into question. Second, the United Nations did not authorize the initial strike because there was some doubt as to whether the war was justifiable as self-defense or if it was an act of unprovoked aggression. In any case, in the next two months, the campaign managed to complete one of its objectives—removing the Taliban from power—but almost eight years later, bin Laden is still at large and al-Qaeda is arguably stronger than it was before.

By December 2001 the Taliban had been driven from power in Afghanistan, and the U.N. sent an international coalition of peacekeeping forces to maintain security in the country. During the main part of the campaign, the Taliban was pushed out of the major cities and took refuge in the vast network of mountains and caves in Afghanistan and possibly in Pakistan as well. Starting about 2003, there was evidence that the Taliban was slowly recouping its strength, and U.S. and international forces have been battling an insurgency ever since.

The Taliban started to reorganize into smaller groups and execute coordinated attacks on American and international troops. Over the years, these attacks have become more technologically advanced and more effective. In addition, by about 2005, Afghanistan was producing a vast majority of the world's opium supply, and the illegal drug trade plus a fragile democratic government have increased instability in the region. For many years, the War in Afghanistan took a back seat to the Iraq War (see next section), but in early 2009 the United States increased its troop presence in Afghanistan in hopes of providing stability to the country and bringing about a faster end to American involvement. The location of Osama bin Laden is still unknown.

THE IRAQ WAR

1991–1998	2001	2002	March	May	2004	2006	2007	2008	2009
U.N. weapons inspectors in Iraq	9/11 attacks	Weapons inspections resume	U.S. invades Iraq	"Mission Accomplished"	U.S. transfers sovereignty to Iraq	Saddam Hussein executed	U.S. troop surge / Iraq in civil war	Troop surge ends	Obama plans troop withdrawal

2003

The War in Afghanistan quickly took second priority to a war in Iraq. As mentioned earlier, following the Persian Gulf War, Iraq was ordered to dismantle its nuclear and biological weapons production capabilities, and a United Nations task force was charged with inspecting weapons facilities to make sure that the job had been completed. These inspections took place between 1991 and 1998. They were halted in December 1998 as the U.S. and Britain launched a four-day bombing campaign against Iraq. The stated purpose of the operation was to "degrade" Saddam

Hussein's weapons capabilities, to "diminish" Iraq's ability to attack its neighbors, and to "demonstrate" the consequences of not cooperating with the U.N. inspectors. The inspections resumed in 2002, but the results were inconclusive.

After the September 11 attacks, there was a lot of support in the United States for President Bush's War on Terrorism. Based on intelligence reports suggesting that Iraq had weapons of mass destruction (WMDs) that were not disclosed to U.N. inspectors and that Hussein's regime was cooperating with the al-Qaeda network, the Bush administration sought authorization for a *pre-emptive* strike against Iraq, that is, a military campaign to prevent Hussein from attacking the U.S., even though no such attack had taken place.

On March 19, 2003, the U.S. and Britain launched a massive invasion of Iraq, and in about six weeks, U.S. forces had succeeded in removing Saddam Hussein from power, though he was not in U.S. custody. On May 1 President Bush announced an end to the major combat, and at the end of the month

he reported that they had found Iraq's WMDs. By the end of the year, Hussein had been captured, but everything went downhill from there.

Although the U.S. had achieved its stated goal and declared the war essentially over, the Bush administration had failed to foresee what Iraq would look like after the war. To begin with, although many Iraqis were unhappy under Hussein's dictatorship, not all of them were, and the U.S. faced resistance from Hussein's supporters. In addition, there were sharp divides between members of different religions in the country, and as a new government was being established, there were violent conflicts over who would lead the nation. These conditions created an extremely volatile situation, and U.S. soldiers were attacked frequently by members of political and religious militias.

Doubts about the reasons for the war also started to surface. First, although Bush had told the American people that WMDs had been found in Iraq, it turned out not to be true—no WMDs were found, and a report was released showing that Iraq never had them. There was also no evidence that Hussein was cooperating with al-Qaeda prior to the invasion (although in the years following, al-Qaeda established a significant presence in Iraq), and Bush admitted that Iraq had nothing to do with the events of 9/11. To the American people, it started to look like either the pre-war intelligence had been faulty or the Bush administration had given misinformation as the justification for going to war.

Meanwhile, the violence in Iraq escalated to the level of a civil war, and the United States could not pull out its troops because the Iraqi military under the newly established government was not yet ready to handle the unrest. Bombings took place almost every day, and the Iraq insurgency slowly became more advanced and more able to execute attacks on U.S. forces as well as on members of rival religious groups. At the end of 2006, after a drawn-out trial that more resembled a circus, Saddam Hussein was found guilty of crimes against humanity and executed.

There had been many calls from the Iraqi government, the American people, and members of the U.S. Congress for the administration to announce a timetable for the withdrawal of the troops, which Bush refused on the basis that setting a timetable would only serve to encourage the enemy. At the beginning of 2007, President Bush announced that more troops would be sent to Iraq to help quell the increasing violence that had taken over the country. This decision led to even more discontentment with the war, and Americans started to feel not only that they had been misled by their government but also that the reputation of the United States internationally was being damaged. There were antiwar demonstrations in many cities, reminiscent of the protests against the Vietnam War. In the first five years of the conflict, about 4,000 American troops and an undetermined number of Iraqis (some estimates top one million) lost their lives, and hundreds of billions of dollars were spent on a war that, like Vietnam, seemed not to be fulfilling its stated purpose of preserving peace and democracy.

The troop surge ended in July 2008, by which time the violence in Iraq had decreased significantly. There also seemed to be signs of improvement in the country. As of early 2009, newly elected President Barack Obama was considering options to bring the American troops home. The full effects of the U.S. actions in Iraq will probably not be properly understood for many years to come.

This chapter has shown how the various military conflicts in which the United States has been involved have shaped the growth of the country. From the Revolutionary War, which gave birth to the nation, to the War on Terrorism, which has redefined the foreign policy of the U.S., each conflict has had a significant impact on the sentiments of the American people as well as on the reputation of the United States in the international community. In the next chapter, we will take a closer look at some of the presidents and leaders who have also contributed to the development of the United States of America.

★ Appy, Christian G. *Patriots: The Vietnam War Remembered from All Sides*. New York: Viking Penguin, 2003.

★ Brogan, Hugh. *The Penguin History of the USA: New ed.* London: Penguin Books, 2001.

★ Catton, Bruce. *The Civil War*. New York: Mariner Books, 1960.

★ Ellis, Joseph J. *American Creation: Triumphs and Tragedies in the Founding of the Republic*. New York: Alfred A. Knopf, 2007.

★ Enstad, Nan. *Ladies of Labor, Girls of Adventure*. New York: Columbia University Press, 1999.

★ Gilbert, Martin. *The Second World War: A Complete History*. New York: Henry Holt and Company, 1989.

★ Hahn, Steven. *A Nation under Our Feet: Black Political Struggles in the Rural South from Slavery to the Great Migration*. Cambridge, Massachusetts: Belknap Press, 2005.

★ Halberstam, David. *The Coldest Winter: America and the Korean War*. New York: Hyperion, 2007.

★ Howe, Daniel Walker. *What Hath God Wrought: The Transformation of America, 1815–1848*. New York: Oxford University Press, 2007.

★ McCullough, David. *1776*. New York: Simon & Schuster, 2005.

★ McPherson, James. *Battle Cry of Freedom: The Civil War Era (Oxford History of the United States)*. New York: Oxford University Press, 1988.

★ Meyer, G. J. *A World Undone: The Story of the Great War, 1914 to 1918*. New York: Delacorte Press, 2007.

★ Middlekauff, Robert. *The Glorious Cause: The American Revolution, 1763–1789*. New York: Oxford University Press, 2007.

★ Ricks, Thomas E. *Fiasco: The American Military Adventure in Iraq*. New York: Penguin, 2006.

★ Shlaes, Amity. *The Forgotten Man: A New History of the Great Depression*. New York: Harper Perennial, 2008.

Chapter Two • Recap Quiz

1. Name at least one of the Civil War battles that was fought on Northern (Union) soil.

2. The Stamp Act was one of many irritants that led to which American war?

3. Which American general (and later president) defeated the British in the Battle of New Orleans in 1815?

4. Which state became part of the U.S. after gaining its independance from Mexico?

5. Who assassinated President Lincoln shortly after the end of the Civil War?

6. Who was President of the United States when America entered World War I?

7. Who was President of the United States when America dropped two atomic bombs on Japan, an act which led directly to the end of World War II?

8. The fighting that would lead to the Vietnam War originally started when Vietnam was a colony of which European nation?

ANSWERS TO QUIZ TWO

1- Gettysburg, Antietam   2- the Revolutionary War   3- Andrew Jackson

4- Texas   5- John Wilkes Booth   6- Woodrow Wilson

7- Harry Truman   8- France

CHAPTER THREE

AMERICA'S GREATEST

Presidents and Leaders

Several of the
nation's leaders are
remembered for the
manner in which they
rose to the challenges of
the day—with courage,
skill, and vigor.

MOUNT RUSHMORE NATIONAL MEMORIAL

Mount Rushmore National Memorial, located in southwestern South Dakota, features the heads of United States presidents George Washington, Thomas Jefferson, Theodore Roosevelt, and Abraham Lincoln carved into a granite bluff. The massive sculpture was carved into the rim of Mount Rushmore 500 feet above the valley floor. Each head is about 60 feet tall.

*We hold these truths to be sacred and undeniable;
that all men are created equal and independent,
that from that equal creation they derive rights inherent and inalienable,
among which are the preservation of life, and liberty, and the pursuit of
happiness.*

excerpt from a rough draft of the Declaration of Independence
THOMAS JEFFERSON
1743–1826

*A man who is good enough to shed his blood for the country
is good enough to be given a square deal afterwards.
More than that, no man is entitled to, and less than that no man shall have.*

THEODORE ROOSEVELT
1858–1919

*And so, my fellow Americans:
ask not what your country can do for you—ask what you can do for your
country.*

JOHN FITZGERALD KENNEDY
1917–1963

THE CONCEPT OF GREATNESS

What does it mean to be *great*? Does greatness lie in how one is judged in one's time or in how one is remembered? Is it a measure of how a person behaves or of how that behavior affects others? Is greatness a property of an individual or does it arise out of a given situation? Can you be great but unpopular?

Since the late 1800s, Americans have perceived themselves as living in a great nation, and the United States has occupied a leadership role in the world. The American form of government has served as a model for many modern democracies. The United States was instrumental in preserving the free world through the devastation of two world wars. Many great scientific and medical breakthroughs of the twentieth century are products of American imagination. America was the first nation to put a man on the moon and to land an unmanned spacecraft on Mars. Americans worked on the development of the automobile, the television, and the computer, which have revolutionized modern life. The U.S. military continues to be technologically superior to any other in the world. These accomplishments have

only been possible through the work of great men and women.

Of course, the United States has problems. There is poverty and crime, social injustice and racial intolerance. The leaders of the country have worked hard to learn from the mistakes of the past and to correct problems as they arise. The American experiment—the creation of a system of self-government in which all people are equal—is still a work in progress. But, by and large, it is an experiment that was conceived and has been kept running by the work of many great men and women who have committed their lives to its success.

The concept of greatness is, of course, subjective and prone to bias. Historically, we have come to regard several presidents from the 1700s and 1800s as great. Although most Americans consider George Washington and Abraham Lincoln to be great men, it is difficult to get people to agree about the greatness of any of America's post–World War II presidents. Is that because the leaders of today are inferior to those of the past, or has our concept of greatness changed? Some people suggest that we look back on early leaders through "rose-colored glasses," remembering only their successes and their strong points while minimizing their personal and political failures. In contrast, we tend to judge contemporary figures much more harshly, excluding them from greatness based on flaws that we overlook in historical figures.

On the other hand, perhaps we judge leaders of the past on the basis of their accomplishments and leaders of today according to their ideology. For many Democrats, John F. Kennedy and Bill Clinton deserve to be on the list of greatest American presidents, whereas to Republicans, Ronald Reagan surely belongs among their number. A recent poll, voted on by more than 2 million people, named Ronald Reagan as the "greatest American"—from a list that included Abraham Lincoln and George Washington as well as Tom Cruise and Oprah Winfrey. Meanwhile, in other recent polls of who was the "greatest president," Reagan didn't even make the top ten!

The United States has come a long way since the signing of the Declaration of Independence, and that growth has not always been a steady process. There have been dramatic spurts during the administrations of particular presidents when America changed drastically from what it had been previously. There have also been certain periods when the nation seemed to be moving in reverse. In this chapter, we review six political leaders who not only have been instrumental in the development of the country but whose contributions continue to shape American society and character today. The men discussed in this chapter are mostly the "usual suspects," but they provide a basis from which current and future leaders may be assessed.

GEORGE WASHINGTON (1732–1799)

George Washington, the first President of the United States of America, grew up in Virginia as the son of a wealthy farmer. He began working as a surveyor and mapmaker. He came to the attention of the King of England for his leadership in a battle in the French and Indian War, and at age twenty-three he was promoted to commander-in-chief of the Virginia militia. Washington started his political career as a member of the House of Burgesses, the colonial legislature of Virginia. He was later elected to the First and Second Continental Congresses, which led to the writing of the Declaration of Independence and eventually the formation of the American system of government.

Washington's life serves to demonstrate that men are not always born into greatness—sometimes a particular situation is thrust upon them and they find themselves in a position to influence the outcome of a significant historical event. Between 1775 and his death in 1799, Washington participated in nearly all of the activities that gave birth to the United States. He did so not without difficulties and occasional setbacks, but ultimately he achieved much success. Without him, it is questionable whether the U.S. would ever have been formed, or whether it would have had a foundation strong enough to survive.

Washington was elected commander-in-chief of the new Continental Army in June 1775, and he did much to turn the disorganized and undisciplined colonial militias into something resembling an efficient military force. He was also instrumental in driving the British army from Boston in March 1776, and his victories undoubtedly gave the colonists the confidence and inspiration to make the bold move of declaring independence in

George Washington
1732–1799

July 1776. At one point, when it looked like all hope was lost for the new country, Washington offered his own money to the troops to increase enlistment—it worked. It was in part Washington's military successes that helped bring France on the side of the colonists, and it was Washington who forced the surrender of British General Cornwallis in Yorktown, Virginia, in 1781, effectively ending the war.

Immediately following the war, there was no structure for a central government, and Washington was concerned that this weakness would lead the newly formed United States to once again become the property of Britain. Many people, particularly in the military, advocated the creation of a monarchy with Washington as king, an idea that he soundly rejected. It was obvious that something had to be done, and in 1787 Washington was chosen as the president of the Constitutional Convention, which drafted the blueprint for the American system of government (see chapter 4). In 1789, Washington was unanimously elected the first President of the United States, and he remains the only president to receive all of the electoral votes. He was re-elected to a second term in 1792, after which he delivered the shortest inauguration speech in history—only 135 words. During the years of his presidency, he helped solidify the American system of government and established a precedent for the role of the president. For example, he refused to run for a third term, and he focused on the will of the people in making important decisions.

George Washington also set the mold for some of the traits we look for in other great leaders. To begin with, although he was born into a well-to-do family, he had many qualities of a self-made man, including a commitment to hard work. Washington proved himself brave in battle and firm in defending the country. Although he was a slaveholder, he made arrangements for the emancipation of his slaves after his wife's death; in fact, he was the only Founding Father to free his slaves.

At the end of the Revolutionary War, the new country was very vulnerable. No one knew whether a democratic nation such as the United States could even survive. It was essential that strong foundations were laid, and George Washington contributed much to laying those foundations upon which the country could continue to grow. Quite possibly, under someone of less dedication and less vision, the United States of America may have been an experiment doomed to failure.

BENJAMIN FRANKLIN (1706–1790)

Benjamin Franklin was a printer, scientist, politician, author, diplomat, and generally interesting character. He is known for his incredible energy and the diversity of his lifetime achievements in a broad range of fields, from politics to American culture. He had relatively little formal education and achieved his success through hard work, resourcefulness, and resiliency.

Franklin was born in Boston, the tenth of seventeen children. His father wanted him to become a clergyman but could not afford the cost of schooling, so he sent Franklin at age twelve to be an apprentice to his brother who was a printer. Franklin eventually left Boston and ended up in Philadelphia, where he bought a newspaper, *The Pennsylvania Gazette*, which became one of the most popular colonial news sources. Franklin was the publisher, but

Benjamin Franklin
1706–1790

also contributed as an author and even drew the first political cartoon! In 1733, he started publishing *Poor Richard's Almanack*, a book of proverbs and personal advice. The book was hugely popular in its time, and many of Franklin's proverbs have become part of American folklore— "A penny saved is a penny earned"; "God helps them that helps themselves"; and "Three may keep a secret, if two of them are dead." He also became involved in public service, helping to establish a fire department, a library, a university, and a hospital in Philadelphia. His autobiography endures as a significant literary work.

In the late 1740s, Franklin retired from the publishing business and turned his attention to the sciences and his inventions. He pioneered scientific work on electricity, and invented the Franklin stove, bifocal spectacles, and the lightning rod, among other things. He was a practical man, and his home was full of innovative ways to make life a little easier. For example, he attached the butter churn to his wife's rocking chair, so that rather than having to spend hours churning the butter by hand, she could simply sit down and rock back and forth.

In 1750 Franklin also became a member of the Pennsylvania legislature, and he spent several years in London as a representative for the colonies. When trouble started brewing between Britain and the colonies, Franklin did his best to smooth things over. As the Revolutionary War started to break out, he returned to Pennsylvania and began to play an active role in the drive for independence. He was a delegate to the Second Continental Congress and helped draft the Declaration of Independence. During the war, he was sent to France to seek military and financial aid, and he became enormously popular with the French people for his wit and his manner of dress. Franklin was also instrumental in helping to negotiate peace with Britain at the end of the war and was one of the framers of the U.S. Constitution. At the age of eighty-four, one of his last public acts was to sign a petition against slavery.

Like Washington, Franklin helped to define the American character and the traits we consider praiseworthy and commendable. Starting at a young age, he pulled himself out of poverty to achieve both financial and political success. As such, Franklin was the embodiment of the original "American Dream," the belief that for those with courage, resourcefulness, and creativity, there are few limits to the success that can be achieved. He was admired for his sense of humor and his wit. He was also a brave man (as were the other signers of the Declaration of Independence)—at the time the document was written, the signers had reason to fear that if the colonists did not win the Revolutionary War, they could be hanged as traitors.

Franklin also serves as a model for American diplomacy. He possessed a friendliness and amicability which helped persuade other countries, notably France, to support the colonists in their struggle for independence. Franklin's efforts were critical to fostering a diplomatic climate in which the United States could be established and survive.

ABRAHAM LINCOLN (1809–1865)

Many people agree that Abraham Lincoln is America's greatest president. Though his life was full of a great deal of suffering, and at least as many defeats as victories, Lincoln rose up and emerged as a powerful force when America needed one most. Respected through the generations and throughout the world, Lincoln has

Abraham Lincoln
1809–1865

come to stand for the very best of American principles and values—honesty, integrity, wisdom, dedication, and perseverance.

Lincoln was born into extreme poverty in Kentucky in 1809. Through dedication and hard work, he managed to acquire a mostly self-taught education which enabled him to serve as a lawyer in Illinois in the 1830s and 1840s. He loved to read, and he studied history as well as the ideals of former American and world leaders. He found much inspiration in the life and leadership of George Washington. In his early life, Lincoln held a variety of

jobs, from log splitter to store clerk to a very brief stint as a military man.

In 1832, he ran for a seat in the Illinois House of Representatives—he lost. Two years later, he ran again and won. He was re-elected to the state legislature three times. Lincoln took his first public stand on slavery in 1837—he was against the practice, but he was also against the views of extreme abolitionist groups, which he felt augmented the problem rather than solved it. In 1846, Lincoln was elected to the U.S. Congress; he served only one term, after which he returned to Illinois to practice law.

In 1854, Lincoln decided it was time to re-enter the political scene. Congress had passed the Kansas–Nebraska Act, admitting both states to the Union and declaring that the question of slavery could be decided by the states themselves. Lincoln found this act, which was authored by Illinois Democrat Stephen Douglas, unacceptable. In 1856, Lincoln became a member of the new Republican Party, which was formed to stop the expansion of slavery.

Lincoln rose to national attention in 1858, when he ran against Stephen Douglas for a seat in the U.S. Senate. He lost the election, but the two men engaged in a series of debates that remain important pieces of American political literature. The Lincoln–Douglas debates solidified his reputation as a leader against slavery and in favor of democracy and civic duty. It would have been difficult to imagine at that time, probably even for

Md. Allan Pinkerton, President Lincoln, and Major Gen. John A. McClernand, Antietam, October 3rd, 1862.

Lincoln himself, that two years later he would be elected president and that the remainder of his life would be dedicated to the bloodiest of all American wars.

Like George Washington, Abraham Lincoln emerged just as the country was in dire need of a strong leader. With the Southern states having seceded from the Union, Lincoln had two choices: he could sit back and watch the country be split in two, or he could wage a war to reunite it. As seen in chapter 2, he chose the second route. Desperate times call for desperate measures, and Lincoln took some extreme emergency actions—among other things, he instituted martial law in some parts of the country and temporarily suspended certain legal rights. Although some of these emergency measures were illegal, Lincoln believed that they were necessary because of the dire straits that the country was in.

Lincoln worked to rally Northerners behind the cause of preserving the Union, and later behind the cause of abolishing slavery, which was controversial even in the free North. American democracy was still an experiment, and the Civil War brought up questions as to whether any large nation could hold together through compromise among elected politicians drawn from very different regions and who were representing people with very different ideologies and beliefs. Ultimately, Lincoln's work and dedication to preserving the Union at all costs saved the country from disintegration. To many, he became the symbol of the Union, and he remains a powerful symbol of American democracy.

Lincoln was assassinated by John Wilkes Booth on April 14, 1865. The tragedy of his death has only served to augment the contributions he made during his lifetime. He committed his life to serving the nation, and the stress and long hours of determined effort clearly took a toll on him, as evidenced by his appearance in photographs from the date of his first election to the final days of the war. He could not have imagined the large number of lives that would be lost in the Civil War, and these deaths weighed heavily upon his conscience. Lincoln's life was also marked by a good deal of personal tragedy—his mother died when he was a young boy, his wife was notoriously difficult, only one of his four children survived to adulthood, and he himself was given to bouts of depression and a lack of self-confidence.

Abraham Lincoln is a different sort of American hero than George Washington or Benjamin Franklin. He was not an accomplished military man or an international figure.

President Abraham Lincoln's box at Ford's Theater, Washington, D.C.

He is known as a self-sacrificing leader whose strong but steady hand and level head guided the country through difficult times. He was a self-made man who, through hard work and dedication, pulled himself up from humble beginnings. He was also a very well-read and intelligent man who left behind a great body of writing that continues to influence many other American and world leaders to this day. He helped the country redefine itself as truly "united" states. Lincoln's early death probably hindered the nation in its attempt to recover from the war, as no leader was able to fill his shoes (size 14!). Indeed, it would take almost a century for his vision of America to become a reality—a nation where all men truly are considered equal.

THEODORE ROOSEVELT (1858–1919)

In the decades after Lincoln, as has happened several times throughout U.S. history, the country had a series of "caretaker" presidencies. There were, of course, many issues to be dealt with, particularly in the Reconstruction Era, but by and large America's government was concerned with holding down the fort and the day-to-day processes of survival and growth. The world in the later part of the 1800s was changing rapidly—the Industrial Revolution was spreading, European nations were becoming friendlier with each other, and the U.S. was continuing to expand. The country was becoming a more powerful nation, one that could compete on an international level.

Theodore Roosevelt may appear an unlikely candidate for greatness, particularly alongside George Washington and Abraham Lincoln. He was not born into poverty, he was educated at Harvard, and he was a great advocate of strenuous physical activity. Before becoming president following the assassination of President William McKinley and subsequently being elected to his own term, Roosevelt's public service included being the police commissioner of New York City, the governor of New York,

Theodore Roosevelt
1858–1919

and the assistant secretary of the Navy. He earned notoriety for his military record in the Spanish–American War.

Roosevelt's contribution to America was complex, involving both concrete modifications to the system of government as well as intangible changes to the image of the American leader in the early part of the twentieth century. Under Roosevelt, the role of the presidency was strengthened, and he extended the influence of government into new areas, particularly in the business and economic sectors. For

Theodore Roosevelt and the father of the modern environmental conservation movement, John Muir, on Glacier Point, Yosemite Valley, California.

example, he broke up business monopolies and passed legislation controlling railroad rates and establishing food and drug inspection. An outdoorsman, Roosevelt also took the first steps toward the conservation of land and natural resources. Although he did not have a particularly favorable opinion of American Indians, he was seen as helping to advance the cause of equality among black Americans.

On the international scene, Roosevelt helped bring the United States into prominence as a world leader. He was the first to use an international court that had been set up to resolve disputes between countries, and he worked to start the building of the Panama Canal. He also helped negotiate an end to the Russo–Japanese War, for which he was awarded the Nobel Peace Prize in 1906. His policies of intervention in the affairs of other nations were not always popular, but they certainly enlarged the sphere of America's influence. Even after he left the White House, Roosevelt continued to champion socially and politically responsible government.

Despite all of these accomplishments, perhaps the one he will be most remembered for, at least in American popular culture, is a hunting story in which he refused to shoot a bear cub that had been caught and tied to a tree. The story inspired a political cartoon, which in turn inspired an enterprising shop owner to construct a small stuffed animal. Children around the world have been playing with "Teddy bears" ever since.

WOODROW WILSON (1856–1924)

Woodrow Wilson is perhaps not the best known of American presidents. He successfully led the country through World War I and helped to hammer out the peace treaty ending the war, though many of his ideas were eventually rejected. He also started the first attempt at an international organization, the League of Nations. Although this initial attempt failed, it laid the groundwork for the United Nations, which would be formed after World War II with the goal of bringing countries together to prevent future wars. Overall, the verdict of history has treated him favorably and suggested that he was ahead of his time in many of his ideals and objectives.

Wilson is one of the most highly educated and intellectual men who have ever been elected to the U.S. presidency. He graduated from Princeton and the University of Virginia Law School, and earned his Ph.D. at Johns Hopkins University. He was a professor of political science and became the president of Princeton in 1902. Wilson was elected Governor of New Jersey in 1910, and was elected to two terms of office as President of the United States starting in 1912.

During his first term, he carried out a variety of reforms, including the Federal Reserve Act of 1913, which established America's central banking system. He also passed legislation putting restrictions on big business and ensuring fair treatment of the working class, such as imposing an eight-hour workday for certain industries. Wilson won re-election on the slogan "He kept us out of the war," but soon after taking office for the second time, he asked Congress for a declaration of war against

Woodrow Wilson
1856–1924

Germany. Thus, he spent half of his second term fighting the war and the other half trying to prevent it from happening again.

Wilson's most ambitious undertaking came at the end of the war. In 1918, he made a speech to Congress laying out "Fourteen Points" that he believed were essential for maintaining postwar peace. Among other things, it called for the establishment of a League of Nations—an international community to prevent future wars. He led the American peace delegation to Paris to end the war. In the end, Wilson proved to be far more influential outside the United States than within it; he succeeded in getting the League of Nations adopted and started at the Paris Peace Conference in 1919, but he could not convince the U.S. Senate to allow the United States to join. Without America's participation, the League of Nations struggled for survival and ultimately failed. Wilson was awarded the Nobel Peace Prize in 1919 for his negotiation efforts after the war.

Wilson devoted himself zealously to the cause, even touring the nation to explain the importance of the League. During the tour, he collapsed from exhaustion and soon after suffered a massive stroke. Although he completed his term of office, he retired from public life and died three years later, in 1924.

Wilson has been criticized for being inflexible in his idealism and lacking political savvy—the ability to compromise when necessary and to persuade others to cooperate with him. However, his ideals were realized about twenty-five years later when the United Nations opened its doors. Like Lincoln, Wilson did not live to see the full impact of his contributions to the country, and it would take another world war before the United States would realize the value of what Wilson had worked to achieve.

FRANKLIN D. ROOSEVELT (1882–1945)

Franklin D. Roosevelt (a distant cousin of Theodore Roosevelt) is the only president to have been elected to four terms in office (something no longer possible under American law). His administration presided over two of the biggest crises in American history: the Great Depression and World War II. Like Wilson, Franklin Roosevelt was very well educated, having graduated from Harvard University and Columbia Law School. His wife, Eleanor, was also intelligent and well-educated, and she played an important role during and

Franklin D. Roosevelt
1882–1945

Roosevelt signing the Declaration of War against Japan in 1941.

after his administration as an advocate for civil rights.

Roosevelt was stricken with polio in 1921, and was disabled for the rest of his life. During his presidency he struggled to maintain an image of sturdiness, but he could never again walk unaided. He was usually photographed by the press in positions where his wheelchair or leg braces were not visible, and many Americans had no idea that their president had a physical disability.

His political career began in the New York State Senate in 1910, and he was re-elected in 1912. He worked under Woodrow Wilson as the assistant secretary of the Navy, and was elected Governor of New York in 1928. When the stock market crashed in 1929 setting off the Great Depression, Roosevelt made his name as a liberal reformer, instituting several relief programs. In 1932, he was elected President of the United States on the promise of a "New Deal" to help the country out of its economic trouble. Roosevelt inherited an extremely bleak situation—America was weakened by massive unemployment and a shortage of key resources, while at the same time tensions were growing in Europe.

On the home front, Roosevelt acted aggressively to help Americans who were suffering most from the depression, and in doing so, he forever changed the role of the federal government with regard to social responsibility. Roosevelt's New Deal programs implemented broad reforms to create jobs and rebuild the U.S. economy and financial system. He worked to help farms and industries, and created Social Security which established a social safety net. Although it took a long time for the country to climb out of the Depression, by the end of the 1930s, most Americans had seen their lives improve and they continued to support Roosevelt through his future terms in office.

Roosevelt was initially determined to keep the U.S. out of World War II, but once American involvement became inevitable, he was an effective statesman

Roosevelt's funeral procession with horse-drawn casket, traveling down Pennsylvania Avenue on April 24, 1945.

and military leader. He mobilized industry for military production and helped maintain a strong alliance with Britain and the Soviet Union to keep the Allied cause united.

Like Lincoln and Wilson, Franklin Roosevelt would not live to see the full impact his policies had on America's political and social scenes. Having struggled with ill health for many years, Roosevelt's condition declined rapidly starting in 1944, and he died of a cerebral hemorrhage in April 1945, several months before the end of World War II. Roosevelt was an extraordinary man who helped Americans display the courage necessary to make it through the tough times of the Great Depression. He showed people that there was a light at the end of the tunnel. In terms of political contributions, he expanded the role of government to include social welfare programs and created methods of economic stimulus that have been used since his time.

Suggested Reading

★ Flexner, James Thomas. *Washington: The Indispensable Man*. New York: Back Bay Books, 1994.

★ Goodwin, Doris Kearns. *No Ordinary Time—Franklin & Eleanor Roosevelt: The Home Front in World War II*. New York: Touchstone, 1994.

★ Goodwin, Doris Kearns. *Team of Rivals: The Political Genius of Abraham Lincoln*. New York: Simon & Schuster, 2005.

★ Isaacson, Walter. *Benjamin Franklin: An American Life*. New York: Simon & Schuster, 2003.

★ Morris, Edmund. *The Rise of Theodore Roosevelt*. New York: Modern Library, 2001. First published 1979 by Coward, McCann & Geoghegan.

★ Thompson, J. A. *Woodrow Wilson*. Harlow, United Kingdom: Pearson Longman, 2002.

1. In what year was George Washington elected president for the first time?

2. Who wrote *Poor Richard's Almanack*?

3. Theodore Roosevelt became famous for his military record in which war?

4. The League of Nations was an ambitious proposal for international cooperation championed by which American president?

5. What was the name given collectively to Franklin Roosevelt's social programs for dealing with the Great Depression?

ANSWERS TO QUIZ THREE

1- 1789   2- Benjamin Franklin   3- the Spanish–American War

4- Woodrow Wilson   5- the New Deal

THE EVOLUTION
of American Government

The American experiment gave rise to a unique system of self-government. The structure of that government, and its founding principles, ensure certain rights and freedoms to all American citizens.

THE STATUE OF LIBERTY

The Statue of Liberty is a monumental sculpture that symbolizes freedom throughout the world. Its formal name is "Liberty Enlightening the World," and it was given to the United States by France in 1886. The iron frame was devised by French engineer Gustave Alexandre Eiffel, who also built the Eiffel Tower in Paris. The statue is perhaps best known for its symbolic role in greeting immigrants arriving in New York Harbor.

*The Constitution, in all its provisions,
looks to an indestructible Union composed of indestructible States.*

SALMON PORTLAND CHASE
1808–1873

Our country is the world—our countrymen are all of mankind.

WILLIAM LLOYD GARRISON
1805–1879

We must be the great arsenal of democracy.

FRANKLIN D. ROOSEVELT
1882–1945

The history of the United States is a record of individual events that have affected the lives of people living in the country and also left the country changed both internally and in terms of its position in the world. Often, these have been dramatic events, such as wars, territorial expansion, and economic booms and depressions. However, the United States has also been shaped by a more subtle growth and refinement of the system of government and the rights of citizens. This chapter reviews the government of the United States and how that system came to be developed.

The United States did not suddenly spring into existence on July 4, 1776. Rather, like a 230-year-old tree, it has developed and expanded throughout its existence. Parts of the current system have remained essentially unchanged since it was put into place by the Founding Fathers, while other elements have grown well beyond what those men envisioned in their original concept of the nation.

The Founding Fathers of the United States produced three very important documents toward the end of the eighteenth century.

★ The Declaration of Independence
★ The Constitution of the United States of America
★ The Bill of Rights

These documents formed the basis of the great American experiment—a system of self-government in which all people are equal. They outline the rights and freedoms to which all Americans are entitled, as well as provide for the

Signing of the Declaration of Independence, painting by John Trumbull in the U.S. Capitol.

democratic system by which leaders are elected. There are a great many aspects of government as it functions today that were not specifically mentioned in the founding documents. These aspects have come about as a result of laws being enacted at the federal or state levels. New laws are being enacted all the time, revising the concept of America and how it operates in response to the changing realities of the modern world.

THE DECLARATION OF INDEPENDENCE

Once the Revolutionary War was underway and it appeared that the colonies could not resolve their differences with England, the Continental Congress met to authorize a formal declaration of independence which would create a new country called the United States of America. Thomas Jefferson, along with a committee, wrote the document, and Congress approved it on July 4, 1776.

In and of itself, the Declaration of Independence does not establish the American form of government. The second paragraph lays down what have come to be thought of as the quintessential American rights, and asserts the right of the people to create a new government when these rights have been abandoned:

We hold these truths to be self-evident, that all men are created equal, that they are endowed by their Creator with certain unalienable Rights, that among these are Life, Liberty and the pursuit of Happiness.—That to secure these rights, Governments are instituted among Men, deriving their just powers from the consent of the governed,—That whenever any Form of Government becomes destructive of these ends, it is the Right of the People to alter or to abolish it, and to institute new Government, laying its foundation on such principles and organizing its powers in such form, as to them shall seem the most likely to effect their Safety and Happiness.

These sentences not only establish the framework for freedom in American society, they also declare a fundamental right of self-government. The authors wanted to make it clear that the authority of government in the United States would come from the citizens themselves. Though this is not such a radical idea today, in the 1700s it was very cutting-

The Declaration of Independence

edge. Most countries were ruled by monarchs (kings or queens), and freedom was not an element of most people's lives. In the beginning, there were serious doubts that a democracy such as the U.S. was proposing could even survive.

Most of the rest of the Declaration of Independence is a list of grievances against King George III of England. The Founding Fathers wanted to make absolutely clear, in the historical record, all of the reasons they had for breaking free from their mother country. The grievances included Britain forcing the colonies to house and feed British troops, cutting off trade between America and certain parts of the world, imposing taxes without consent of the colonies, and depriving the colonists of the right to trial by jury. The Declaration also points out how hard the colonists tried to make their grievances heard, with no result. King George is labeled as a tyrant, and his tyrannical behavior was the justification for the actions of the colonists. The final paragraph contains the new status that is being declared:

We, therefore, the Representatives of the united States of America, in General Congress, Assembled, appealing to the Supreme Judge of the world for the rectitude of our intentions, do, in the Name, and by Authority of the good People

"Making the Flag" by Jean Louis Gerome Ferris

of these Colonies, solemnly publish and declare, That these United Colonies are, and of Right ought to be Free and Independent States ...

Thus, the Founding Fathers declared the existence of a new country—that was the easy part. Then came the hard part—establishing a new system of government that abided by all of the ideals put forth in the Declaration of Independence. The Founding Fathers created a blueprint in 1787, and the American system of democracy has been under construction ever since.

THE CONSTITUTION OF THE UNITED STATES OF AMERICA

The Constitution is both the blueprint and the rulebook for the United States government. It was drafted in 1787, and

Congress declared it to be in effect the following year, after nine of the thirteen original states formally ratified it. Almost immediately after the Constitution was ratified, Congress began building new provisions into it. The first ten amendments, which were enacted in 1791, are known as the Bill of Rights. They outline the basic rights guaranteed to every U.S. citizen. Other amendments have been added over the years, twenty-seven to be exact, but this is not an easy process. Amendments must first be passed by two-thirds of Congress and then ratified by three-quarters of the states.

The body of the Constitution contains seven articles.

★ Article I: Organization, powers, and procedures for Congress (the legislative branch)

★ Article II: Election, powers, and duties of the president and vice president (the executive branch)

★ Article III: Powers and jurisdiction of the Supreme Court and inferior courts to be established by Congress (the judicial branch)

★ Article IV: Relations among states, and how new states may be admitted

★ Article V: How the Constitution can be amended

★ Article VI: Public debts and the supremacy of the Constitution

★ Article VII: How the Constitution must be ratified

The first three articles of the Constitution establish three branches of government: legislative, executive, and judicial. These branches have unique responsibilities: the legislative branch (Congress) makes laws, the executive branch (the president) executes laws, and the judicial branch *interprets* laws. The three branches were created based on the principle of a "separation of powers." The framers of the Constitution were concerned that if too much power was given to one branch, the government would resemble the monarchy that they were busy fighting to be free of. The Constitution establishes a system of federalism, in which power is divided between a central authority (the federal government) and smaller political units (the states).

The framework of government described by the first three articles of the Constitution has not changed significantly since it was first adopted. The following paragraphs summarize the present structure and function of the U.S. federal government.

The legislative branch is divided into two chambers: the Senate and the House of Representatives. The Senate is designed to give equal power to all states. Two senators are elected from each state, regardless of the state's size or population, and senators serve six-year terms. Membership in the House of Representatives, on the other hand, is based on each state's population. Large states, like California, can have more than fifty representatives, whereas small

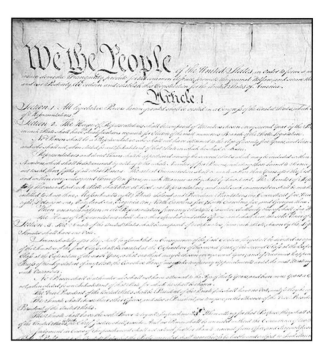

The Constitution of the United States of America.

states, such as Vermont, may have only one. The number of representatives for each state can change if there are large shifts in population. There are currently 435 members of the House of Representatives, though that number has changed over time. Representatives serve two-year terms.

Although the two chambers of Congress operate in similar ways, they also each have some unique responsibilities. The Senate must approve all appointments made by the president, for example, for members of the Cabinet, the Supreme Court, and ambassadors to foreign countries. Meanwhile, the House of Representatives is responsible for initiating all bills related to how the government spends its money.

The President of the United States is elected by the people every four years.

When the Constitution was first enacted, there were no term limits for presidents, but in 1951, the Twenty-second Amendment set a limit of two terms. The president is the head of state, the chief lawmaker, and the commander-in-chief of the U.S. army. The vice president is elected along with the president and becomes president in the event that the president should die or leave office before the end of the term. The vice president also leads the Senate and may cast a vote in that chamber of Congress in the event of a tie.

The Constitution also establishes a Supreme Court, which has authority over all other courts in the country. Decisions made by lower courts may be appealed to and overturned by the Supreme Court. The Supreme Court mainly hears cases involving the Constitution; for example, if a state passes a law that some people think is not in keeping with the Constitution, that law may be examined by the Supreme Court.

In addition to a separation of powers, the Founding Fathers built into the American government a system of "checks and balances"—each branch "checks" the power of the other two branches. For example, laws are passed by Congress, but they must be signed by the president, who also has an option to veto them. If the president vetoes a law, it can still be enacted if it is approved by two-thirds of Congress. Even if a law is enacted, the Supreme Court may decide that it is unconstitutional. The Supreme Court is

still not the last word, however, because the Constitution itself can always be amended. For almost every function of government, there are clearly defined processes by which each branch keeps the other branches from becoming too powerful.

When the country was first beginning, there were huge differences in lifestyles and viewpoints among the original states, for example, about slavery. There were different ways of thinking in Virginia compared with Pennsylvania and New York. When the colonies agreed to merge, they did not want to all be dissolved into one entity, and they did not want all of the power to lie with the federal government. They wanted to be able to deal with their individual needs and

The U.S. Capitol, where Congress convenes, in Washington, D.C.

regional concerns on their own; they did not want their fates to be decided entirely by the rest of the country. Consequently, the Constitution also establishes a division between federal and state powers, or rather it sets limits on what the federal government is allowed to do and leaves the rest to the states. Each state also has a legislative branch, an executive branch (the governor), and a judicial branch of government.

Briefly, the federal government has the power to raise an army, go to war, and enact trade agreements with other nations. It also looks after matters that extend across state lines, such as interstate transportation. The states, on the other hand, look after a great many matters that affect day-to-day elements of public life, including social services, education, public works (state highways, bridges, etc.), and the establishment and regulation of local governments. The states also have their own courts and are able to pass their own laws concerning a broad range of civil and criminal matters. Although there are many similarities in the laws of states, there are some significant differences as well. For example, states have different laws concerning the sale of alcohol. Furthermore, penalties for committing crimes vary from one state to another. Some states still use the death penalty for certain crimes, whereas others have abolished the death penalty altogether. The table on the next page shows some similarities and differences between the powers of state and federal governments.

Federal Government	State Government	Both Levels of Government
Declare war	Establish local governments	Collect taxes
Print money	Issue licenses	Build roads
Regulate trade between states and with other countries	Regulate business within the state	Establish courts
Sign treaties with other countries	Ratify amendments to the U.S. Constitution	Make and enforce laws
Raise an army	Create public school systems	Charter corporations

THE BILL OF RIGHTS

The original ten amendments that make up the Bill of Rights are the shining jewels of the U.S. system of government. They embody the fundamental rights and freedoms guaranteed to all American citizens. It is this document, more than any other, that has served as a model to the world of what a free and democratic society should be.

Interpreting and enforcing the Bill of Rights have been complex and difficult issues throughout history. Even today, court cases continue to be decided based on judicial interpretation of constitutional amendments. Freedom of speech and freedom of the press are provided for in the First Amendment. In practice, the courts must determine what reasonable limitations there are to such rights. For example, although people do have the right to speak their minds, they do not have the right to incite others to overthrow the government or to commit hate crimes. They also do not have the right to use speech to slander or defame another person's reputation. The press has the right to report the truth, with specific limitations. For example, the courts may impose a restriction on the right of the press to report certain information about a case that is being tried. For national security reasons, the government may block certain information from being given to the press or prevent the press from reporting it.

The Bill of Rights

★ First Amendment: Freedom of religion, speech, assembly, and the press, and the right to petition the government

★ Second Amendment: Right to keep and bear arms

★ Third Amendment: Protection of citizens against having to lodge soldiers

★ Fourth Amendment: Protection against unreasonable search and seizure

★ Fifth Amendment: Rights of the accused to due process and to avoid self-incrimination

★ Sixth Amendment: Rights of the accused to a public and speedy trial

★ Seventh Amendment: Right to trial by jury in civil cases

★ Eighth Amendment: Prohibition of excessive bails and fines, and of cruel and unusual punishment

★ Ninth Amendment: Declaration that rights may exist that are not delineated in the Constitution

★ Tenth Amendment: Declaration that powers not delegated to the federal government may be exercised by the states or the people

The Second Amendment remains one of the most contentious. It gives citizens the right to bear arms (guns and other weapons). While most of the fundamental rights in the Bill of Rights are as applicable today as they were more than 200 years ago, some argue that the protections of the Second Amendment do not make sense in today's world. With the many problems that illegal or imprudent use of firearms have caused, certain groups within the country would like to see the Second Amendment repealed or altered. The federal government has restricted people from owning certain types of weapons and may impose more restrictions. In addition, the government punishes those who use firearms illegally.

The Fourth Amendment has also provoked some special concerns. It protects against unreasonable searches and seizures, but the term *unreasonable* has been open to interpretation. Laws have been established to define the precise manner in which searches of persons, homes, or vehicles may be conducted by police during an investigation or an arrest.

Several items in the Bill of Rights deal with how persons accused of crimes must be brought to justice. These provisions sprang from widespread abuse of the courts and prison systems that were common in other parts of the world in the eighteenth century. Prisoners were often given unfair trials, beaten, tortured, subjected to harsh punishments, and held in jail without bail for long periods of time awaiting trial. The Bill of Rights allows for a judicial system whereby persons accused of crimes are presumed innocent until found guilty, and where they are given rights to a fair trial and humane treatment both before and after being convicted.

The first ten amendments to the Constitution

THE GROWTH OF GOVERNMENT

As the size and population of the United States have grown, the government has grown as well, at both the state and federal levels. In the early days, the role of government was much smaller; for example, there was no income tax. Taxes were assessed on some activities such as the importation and sale of goods, but it wasn't until the Sixteenth Amendment was passed in 1913 that the federal government was authorized to impose income taxes.

From the beginning the federal government has maintained a military and enacted treaties with Native Americans,

territories, and foreign governments. However, initially it had very little to do with regulating business within the country or with social programs and conditions. There was no welfare system or unemployment insurance. There were no laws protecting workers or banning unsafe practices. Laws were quickly enacted to designate serious crimes, but the wide range of activities currently considered crimes has emerged gradually over many decades of interaction between the different branches of the state and federal governments.

As these needs have arisen, governments have enacted laws, sometimes on the state level, sometimes as amendments to the Constitution. For example, during the Industrial Revolution when factories were becoming more prevalent, it became necessary to control big business and set

labor standards. Following the Civil War and at other times in the country's history, it became necessary to further protect the rights of Americans as well as better define exactly who was considered an American citizen. More recently it has become necessary to pass laws protecting the environment and regulating transportation.

As mentioned, there have been twenty-seven amendments to the Constitution, some of them dealing with issues that we currently take for granted. Slavery was not officially abolished until 1865, women got the vote in 1920, and the voting age in general was twenty-one until 1971. Now, all people can vote starting at age eighteen. Not all senators were elected by the people until the Seventeenth Amendment in 1913. One amendment was even repealed, which required another amendment! The Eighteenth Amendment, ratified in 1919, prohibited the sale of alcohol. This policy led to more problems than solutions, and it was undone by the Twenty-first Amendment in 1933.

Today, there are wide-ranging laws about business practices, taxation, discrimination, and the invasion of privacy. The Founding Fathers did not create laws against child pornography, drunk driving, or stock market fraud, but it became necessary for Congress to pass laws on all of these issues. As life has become more complicated, government has become more complicated. The good news is that the American system of government is set up so that it can respond to the changing needs of the country and its citizens.

★ O'Connor, Karen and Larry J. Sabato. *American Government: Continuity and Change, 2008 Ed.* Harlow, United Kingdom: Pearson Longman, 2008.

★ Shaffrey, Mary M. and Melanie Fonder. *The Complete Idiot's Guide to American Government, 2nd ed.* New York: Alpha Books, 2005.

Chapter Four • Recap Quiz

1.   What is the name given to the first ten amendments to the U.S. Constitution?

2.   Fill in the blanks in the following famous quotation from the Declaration of Independence: "We hold these truths to be self-evident, that all men are created equal, that they are endowed by their Creator with certain unalienable Rights, that among these are _____ , _____ and the pursuit of _____."

3.   How many articles are contained in the body of the U.S. Constitution?

4.   In order to be passed in spite of a presidential veto, a law must receive the approval of at least _____ of the members of the House of Representatives and the same majority in the Senate.

5.   Freedom of speech, religion, and the press are all guaranteed by which amendment to the Constitution?

ANSWERS TO QUIZ FOUR

1- the Bill of Rights   2- Life, Liberty, Happiness   3- seven

4- two-thirds   5- the First Amendment

AMERICAN HISTORY

since 1945

Since the end of
World War II, the
United States has established
itself as a global superpower
while facing the challenges of
an ever-changing social and
political landscape within
its own borders.

THE WASHINGTON MONUMENT

The Washington Monument, national memorial completed in 1884. Located in Washington, D.C., at the western end of the National Mall, this four-sided stone structure honors George Washington, the first president of the United States. The monument was modeled after a classic Egyptian obelisk. It is 555 feet high and one of the tallest masonry structures in the world.

Some people call me an idealist. Well, that is the way I know I am an American. America is the only idealistic nation in the world.

WOODROW WILSON
1856–1924

America is a system of rugged individualism.

HERBERT HOOVER
1874–1964

At the end of World War II, the United States emerged as a major international power—the country had just helped bring an end to the war by exploding the most destructive device known to humankind. While people around the world were reacting to this awesome display of power, there were many changes taking place in the psychology of the country. Chapter 2 touched on the Cold War and its military consequences worldwide, but the fear of communism had an impact on America's internal politics as well. Women, who had contributed greatly to the war effort by going to work in factories, were ready to redefine their role in society on a permanent basis. The racial prejudice and discrimination that had, in the past, been intertwined with American law (for example, slavery, Indian Removal, and the Chinese Exclusion Act) still needed to be addressed on the social, cultural, and political levels. In short, the opinions of Americans were changing about a lot of things, and the post-war period brought a new set of challenges for the U.S. both at home and on the global scene.

THE START OF THE COLD WAR AND A CHANGING SOCIETY

The end of the Second World War ushered in the Cold War, a bitter rivalry between the United States and the Soviet Union. From the American perspective, the purpose of Cold War policy was to stop the spread of communism, which many Americans felt was a threat to their way of life.

Dwight D. Eisenhower served as Supreme Commander of the Allied Forces in Europe during World War II. As President, his long list of accomplishments include ending the Korean War, the creation of the Interstate Highway System, and maintaining peace with the Soviet Union during the beginning of the Cold War.

One aspect of the Cold War was seen in foreign relations and a buildup of defense capabilities. In 1947, the Truman administration revealed the policy of containment in what became known as the Truman Doctrine. This policy allowed the United States to send aid to countries resisting communism, even if it meant providing money and materials to incompetent or "undesirable" governments, such as a racist regime in South Africa. In 1948, the U.S. government instituted the Marshall Plan providing money and supplies to aid in the reconstruction of Western Europe, which had been heavily damaged during World War II. The Marshall Plan was

not completely altruistic, however, as the government reasoned that stabilizing the economy and improving the standard of living in these devastated countries would make the people less likely to be attracted to the idea of communism. Starting in 1949, the United States began signing mutual defense pacts with other countries, reasoning that the idea of facing the militaries of many countries would curtail the efforts of the Soviet Union to expand its political influence. In the eyes of the American government, any political movement in any country that had any hint of communism was seen as taking orders from Moscow, whether or not the movement was actually associated with the Soviet Union. These policies led directly to U.S. involvement in the Korean and Vietnam Wars.

Worried by the mass destruction capabilities of the United States seen in the bombing of Hiroshima and Nagasaki, the Soviet Union also rushed to develop a nuclear weapon, which it accomplished in 1949. President Truman was equally concerned about America's rival having such an awesome weapon, and authorized the development of a hydrogen bomb, which would be even more destructive than the atomic bomb. Although different leaders would handle the situation differently, the remainder of the Cold War was characterized by an arms race in which the United States and the Soviet Union would try to outdo each other in terms of quantity and destructive capacity of weapons. The arms race was coupled with a "space race," and during this time the U.S. also poured a lot of money into space technology and exploration.

The Cold War would also spread fear of communism inside the United States, and the late 1940s and early 1950s saw what can only be described as a "witch hunt" in various parts of the country. Based on evidence that a Soviet spy network had been operating in the United States quite effectively for some time, President Truman established a domestic loyalty program, whose purpose was to look for subversive people and organizations operating in the government sphere. U.S. government employees, Hollywood producers, actors, artists, and intellectuals were accused of being communists, and the Federal Bureau of Investigation (FBI) kept files on many Americans. Labor unions also came under attack, and it is estimated that security checks were carried out on as many as one in five members of the American workforce. By 1954, the fevered pitch of these accusations had mostly calmed down, and the fight against communism was seen primarily in weapons development, mutual defense pacts, and the sending of financial and military aid to other countries.

The 1950s also ushered in huge changes in the social and political landscapes of the United States. A period of steady economic growth meant that everyone had a little more money to spend, and new products and technologies meant that there were a lot of fun things for people to buy. More people could afford cars, and newer technologies

brought large appliances and televisions into homes across the country. Televisions in turn caused a growth spurt in popular culture, and entertainment personalities like Elvis Presley had a huge impact on the younger generation. As cars became more prevalent, more people moved to suburbs, which began to be filled with inexpensive single-family homes. American families were able to move into their own "cookie-cutter" houses, buy washing machines, and watch *I Love Lucy* while eating T.V. dinners. The American Dream had been reinvented.

The position of women in society was also changing rapidly. During World War II, many women had gone to work in factories, and many of them did not want to return to how things had been before the war. With the men away, women had become more assertive, independent, and capable of taking care of themselves. The government launched an active campaign to convince women that it was their patriotic duty to give up their work and that they would be happier staying at home with the kids. In addition, the increase in ownership of appliances and televisions,

Telephone operators, 1952

along with relocation to suburbs, greatly changed what it meant to be a housewife. The messages women were receiving at this time were often mixed. Women were told by television programs, advertising agencies, and the government that to be a perfect wife and perfect mother was the highest achievement a woman could attain. On the other hand, the image of a "femme fatale" dominated movie screens, and certain jobs—for example, nursing and teaching—came to be dominated by women. Soon, although women were being told that they should be happy cooking and cleaning and mothering, many middle-class women needed to work so the family could maintain its new standard of living. Overall, it was a very confusing time for American families, and American women in particular.

Issues of race were also coming to the forefront of the American landscape. Black men had fought in many wars for the

United States, and black men and women had been contributing to the workforce and the American economy since the first slaves were brought to the New World. Even though slavery was outlawed in 1865 and black men and women had been granted the right to vote, racial inequality still existed in many areas, especially in the South. In the late 1800s, after the emancipation of the slaves, many former slave owners and white supremacists were elected to public office. From then until the mid-twentieth century, many state and local laws were passed that provided for segregation of blacks and whites, under the principle that blacks would be accommodated in a "separate but equal" fashion. Thus, in many parts of the country, blacks were not allowed to be educated at the same schools as whites, could not drink out of the same water fountains, and even had to sit in the back on public buses. Many restaurants had separate tables and restrooms for black and white customers.

In 1954, however, the Supreme Court overturned the decision in regard to public schools, recognizing that "separate" was rarely, if ever, "equal." The next year in Montgomery, Alabama, a black woman named Rosa Parks refused to give up her seat on the bus to a white passenger; she was arrested and put in jail. An association led by Baptist minister Martin Luther King, Jr., organized a boycott of the Montgomery bus system in which about 90% of the black community refused to use public transportation. After about a year (and a great deal of lost revenue for the bus system), the federal district court ruled segregation on buses unconstitutional. (See chapter 6 for a more detailed profile of Dr. Martin Luther King, Jr.)

THE KENNEDY ADMINISTRATION

In 1960, Americans elected a young, charismatic World War II hero and U.S. congressman to the presidency—John F. Kennedy. Kennedy was elected by a very narrow margin on the promise "to get the country moving again." His term in office is marked by two major themes: Cuba and civil rights.

One battle in America's fight against communism took place dangerously close to its shores—in Cuba, where Fidel Castro had set up a communist dictatorship. In early 1960, President Eisenhower agreed to a covert operation to orchestrate an overthrow of Castro. The plan was to train Cuban exiles, drop them in the Bay of Pigs, and hope the invasion would spark an uprising against Castro. The invasion was launched in early 1961, just a few months after Kennedy took office. Unfortunately for the exiles, the Cuban government knew that the attack was coming and managed to defeat the attempt in about three days. The incident caused a rapid deterioration of the relationship between Cuba and the United States.

The following year, 1962, brought an additional confrontation in Cuba, though this time it worked out more favorably for the United States. The U.S. learned that

John F. Kennedy

the Soviet Union was building missile bases in Cuba, and the American government feared that the missiles might be aimed at the U.S. In response, President Kennedy demanded that the missiles be removed and threatened military involvement if they were not. For about two weeks, the United States and the Soviet Union were dangerously close to engaging in nuclear war. In the end, the Soviet Union agreed to remove the missiles from Cuba in exchange for a promise that the United States would not invade the island. Privately, Kennedy also struck a deal with Soviet Union leader Nikita Khrushchev that called for the dismantling of American missiles in Turkey. Kennedy's foreign policy also led to more U.S. money and troops going to support anticommunist forces in Vietnam,

Lyndon Baines Johnson taking the oath of office on Air Force One, shortly after the assassination of John F. Kennedy on November 22, 1963.

but he would not live long enough to see the full impact of the war in that country.

At home, the movement toward racial desegregation was helped along by nonviolent protests and grassroots activism. In some parts of the South, however, race relations turned violent and President Kennedy used U.S. marshals and the National Guard to calm racial tensions. He also pledged to ban racial discrimination from federally funded housing and asked Congress to pass legislation guaranteeing black Americans equal rights to vote, as well as to education and other services. In terms of women's rights, he signed the Equal Pay Act of 1963 making it illegal to pay a woman less for doing the same job as a man, and promised to rid the federal civil service of sexism. Kennedy was also known for his efforts to fight poverty and his support for the space program.

On November 22, 1963, the nation was shocked as President Kennedy was killed by gunfire while his motorcade drove through Dallas, Texas. A rumored communist sympathizer named Lee Harvey Oswald was caught and arrested for the assassination, but while being transferred between prison facilities, Oswald was killed at point-blank range by a Dallas nightclub owner. Although a commission headed by Chief Justice of the Supreme Court Earl Warren concluded that Oswald was the assassin and that he had acted alone, many questions were left unanswered. For example, some evidence suggests that bullets came from multiple directions, which would mean that there was more than one shooter. Oswald maintained his innocence, and was murdered so soon after the Kennedy assassination that it will probably never be known for certain if he killed the president, and (perhaps more importantly) why he did it and if he acted alone.

THE 1960s

The assassination of John F. Kennedy left the White House to Kennedy's vice president, Lyndon B. Johnson. In the year following the assassination, Johnson worked to pass many pieces of legislation that Kennedy supported, including an economic stimulus plan, a policy to reduce poverty, and the Civil Rights Act of 1964 officially outlawing racial segregation. After completing Kennedy's term, Johnson was elected to the presidency for his own term. President Johnson planned a series of reforms he called the Great Society. The programs included providing healthcare insurance to elderly and low income citizens, improving public education, creating more jobs and opportunities for low income Americans, ending racial discrimination at voting polls, and many other reforms. While the economy was prospering, people were supportive of these reforms, but later in the decade the economy started to decline and many Americans were not happy with how their tax dollars were being spent. In addition, the United States was becoming much more involved in the Vietnam War, and much of the money intended for the Great Society programs ended up being redirected to the war effort.

The '60s also brought social and cultural changes. There was considerable disagreement about U.S. involvement in the Vietnam War, and many people participated in antiwar protests and demonstrations. During this time, there was also a movement, mainly among the younger generations, against the social conformity of the 1950s. The term *counterculture* is used to describe younger Americans who took on political causes,

Signing of the Civil Rights Act of 1964.

such as the Vietnam War, feminism, and environmental activism, but also rebelled socially as well. The movement came to be associated with "hippies," who emphasized freedom of expression, listened to protest music, and experimented with drugs.

By the end of the decade, the country was spinning out of control and there was a high degree of civil unrest. The war in Vietnam had been steadily escalating with no end in sight, civil rights leader Martin Luther King, Jr., was assassinated, and race riots had begun to spring up across the country. In an effort to change the course of the country, in 1968 Americans elected Republican Richard Nixon to the presidency.

THE 1970s

President Nixon brought a new face to U.S. foreign relations. In the Cold War, Nixon adopted a policy of *détente*, which basically means an easing of tensions through increased diplomacy. At the time, both China and the Soviet Union were major communist powers. Nixon and his secretary of state, Henry Kissinger, paid a historic visit to China in 1972, setting the stage for a better relationship between China and the U.S. That same year, Nixon visited the Soviet Union and arranged a deal whereby both countries would limit the production of certain nuclear weapons. They also signed a trade agreement and agreed to collaborate on a space program.

In the Vietnam War, Nixon started a policy of *Vietnamization*, according to which the United States would start withdrawing its forces as South Vietnamese troops were trained. This signaled a new approach to fighting communism—the U.S. would support anticommunist movements in other countries, but those other countries were required to provide their own military forces for the effort. The Paris Peace Treaty of 1973 ended U.S. involvement in the war in Vietnam with what Nixon called "peace with honor." However, as mentioned in chapter 2, South Vietnam would soon be taken over by the communist forces of North Vietnam. For the first time, the United States had lost a war.

President Nixon won a landslide victory for a second term of office in 1972; however, soon after the election he became embroiled in a scandal that would forever taint his presidency. Worried that the Democratic Party might gain control of the White House, five men working for the Committee to Re-elect the President (CREEP) and armed with surveillance equipment broke into the headquarters of the Democratic National Convention at the Watergate Hotel in Washington, D.C. It is not known whether Nixon was involved in the break-in itself, but evidence suggests that he was involved in a subsequent cover-up. The administration attempted to block an FBI investigation of the event, and Nixon refused to hand over taped recordings of Oval Office conversations

President Richard Nixon's second term in office (left to right): Secretary of State Henry Kissinger, Nixon, Vice President Gerald Ford, and Chief of Staff Alexander Haig.

until he was ordered to do so by the Supreme Court. When he did release the tapes, there were about seventeen minutes that had been erased. Nixon's dishonesty about what he knew and his attempts to obstruct the investigation rapidly sapped his public image and popularity, and caused overwhelming opposition to mount against him in Congress. On August 4, 1974, Nixon resigned from office while Congress was pursuing impeachment proceedings against him. In a strange twist of events, Nixon's vice president, Spiro Agnew, had also resigned because of a scandal over tax evasion, so on August 9 Gerald Ford, a man who had not been elected to either office, became the thirty-eighth President of the United States.

The 1970s was an uneasy decade for America. The people had lost confidence in their government, and the economy was suffering, largely due to an oil crisis. There were some positives, for example, Nixon established the Environmental Protection Agency and passed several environmental measures such as the Clean Air Act. But, in general, much of the idealism of the '60s had faded, and by and large America still faced internal conflicts and tensions, only this time with more cynicism.

A general sense of dissatisfaction and disillusionment with the Republican Party as a result of the Watergate scandal, coupled with economic problems and frustration with the progress of social reform, helped set the stage for Democrat Jimmy Carter to win the presidency in 1976. Carter, a former Georgia governor and naval officer, campaigned in part on a promise of a more efficient and responsible government based on honesty and integrity.

The Carter administration proved to be a disappointment to many. Although he was known for his emphasis on human rights and was instrumental in brokering a peace deal between Egypt and Israel, little was accomplished by way of improving the domestic situation—the economy continued to flounder and inflation soared. In addition, tensions between the U.S. and parts of the Arab world were deepening, due largely to disagreements on how to manage the world's oil supply. The oil-rich countries of the world instituted an effort to drive up oil prices, for which the U.S. was woefully unprepared. Gas prices in the U.S. more than tripled between 1970 and 1980! Long lines appeared at gas pumps, and occasionally fights broke out as the prices climbed and the supplies became limited.

The incident that doomed the Carter administration, however, was the kidnapping of about sixty people at the American embassy in Iran. In 1979, the *shah*, or king, of Iran was overthrown in the Islamic Revolution, which established an Islamic republic in the country. The shah went into exile, but his health was poor, and he requested medical treatment in the United States, to which the Carter administration agreed. The new government of Iran and its supporters protested America's involvement by seizing hostages from the embassy. American attempts to rescue the hostages failed when U.S. helicopters were caught in a desert dust storm and crashed, and the hostages were kept in captivity for 444 days before being released. Americans, already frustrated with the situation at home, now felt embarrassed that their military was losing its capability to function effectively.

By the end of the 1970s, the *détente* was also failing, and the Cold War was icing over again. Americans were more divided than ever. In addition to the differing views of the Vietnam War, there were other signs of a troubled society—the divorce rate was increasing, and many more people started seeking help from psychologists and psychiatrists. Finally, whereas 1960s counterculture was decidedly liberal, a new conservative faction was gaining popularity in the 1970s. Concerned about moral decline in the country, many people started turning toward religion and a new Christian fundamentalist movement became more active in politics and society.

THE REAGAN–BUSH ERA

In the election of 1980, Americans were looking for a positive change. After a decade of trouble militarily, economically, and socially, people wanted to feel good about their government again, and they found a source of good feeling in former actor Ronald Reagan. Reagan was a staunch conservative—he favored tax cuts, a reduction in the size of government, and an increase in military spending coupled with a decrease in spending for social welfare programs. He was also opposed to abortion, advocated prayer in schools, and supported government promotion of "family values," which appealed to the Christian right. Reagan reduced governmental regulation of business and industry, and weakened environmental restrictions. He was unsympathetic to labor unions, took a hard line on drugs, and favored cheap oil over alternative fuel sources. Overall, Ronald Reagan was a model conservative.

When Reagan took office in 1981, the economy was headed toward a recession. He touted a system called *supply-side economics* in which taxes are cut for the wealthiest portions of society so that more money is available for business and investment; in theory, the money will "trickle down" and benefit the lower and middle classes by creating jobs and increasing incomes. The

Ronald Reagan implemented policies that reversed trends toward greater government involvement in economic and social regulation. He also brought in a new style of presidential leadership, downgrading the role of the president as an administrator and increasing the importance of communication via national news media. He was the oldest person ever to serve as president.

economy rebounded in 1983, but since the government was collecting less revenue from taxes while significantly increasing military defense spending, the federal budget deficit and the national debt soared. In addition, the gap between the rich and the poor was widening.

The increase in military spending was justified by a boost in Cold War rhetoric. Although the 1980s were characterized by a relative peace worldwide, President Reagan announced new weapons programs and a new policy of funding anticommunism movements around the globe. During this time, the U.S. sent money and/or troops to various parts of Africa, Asia, the Middle East, and Latin America. The biggest scandal of Reagan's presidency occurred because of this policy: the Iran-contra scandal. In the early '80s, the government secretly sold weapons to Iran and used the money to help overthrow the ruling party in Nicaragua, both of which activities had been forbidden by Congress.

Throughout the investigation, Reagan claimed that he did not remember anything about the deal being made, and some of his high-level advisors took the blame. Despite criticism over this incident and a few other issues, Reagan remained extremely popular with many Americans, earning him the nickname "the Teflon president," since nothing bad ever seemed to stick. In fact, Reagan remains one of the most popular U.S. presidents of all time.

In 1985, a new leader came to power in the Soviet Union: Mikhail Gorbachev. Recognizing that the Soviet empire could not survive as it was structured, Gorbachev instituted new policies, including a new openness to Western ideas and some limited economic freedom. Two years later, in 1987, Reagan and Gorbachev signed an agreement to reduce production of certain nuclear weapons, effectively putting an end to the Cold War. There are differing opinions about why it happened, but in

Ronald Reagan and George H.W. Bush at the Republican National Convention, 1984.

1989 the Soviet Union collapsed, which for all intents and purposes eliminated the communist threat that Americans had been facing for about forty-five years.

Reagan's popularity and success against communism helped his vice president, George H.W. Bush, be elected to the presidency in 1988. Although he continued many of Reagan's policies and the Soviet Union collapsed during his term in office, Bush was undone by his failure to adequately articulate a clear post–Cold War foreign policy for the United States.

The Persian Gulf War was a mixed victory for President Bush. Americans were happy for a quick military success with relatively few casualties, but they were not so sure they agreed with the justification for going to war. Bush was also hindered by having a Democrat-controlled Congress. Despite his promise of "no new taxes," he had little choice but to sign a budget calling for tax hikes. During his administration, economic growth slowed and the deficit increased, and Bush was less popular with conservative voters than Reagan had been. By the end of his first term in office, it was becoming clear that Americans again needed a change. Twelve years of Republican rule failed to resolve important domestic problems, reduce the national debt, or make life much better for low income or working class Americans. When the young Governor of Arkansas William Clinton ran for office in 1992, he reminded America of the happier and more idealistic days of John F. Kennedy.

THE 1990s AND THE BEGINNING OF THE 21ST CENTURY

In his first few years in office, President Clinton reversed some of the Reagan-era social policies and turned his attention toward healthcare reform and the economy. He put his wife, Hillary Rodham Clinton, in charge of developing a plan to provide healthcare for all Americans. The resulting plan was complicated and faced much criticism in Congress; ultimately, it never got off the ground. His work on the economy, however, made a much bigger impact.

In 1993, President Clinton proposed a deficit-reduction plan that called for tax increases and government spending cuts. Sounding more like a Republican than a Democrat, he worked to reduce the size of government in order to balance the budget. It worked. During his presidency, the U.S. economy was revived by low inflation, a reduced deficit, and rising profits. Unemployment went down and incomes went up. He also worked with Congress to reform the welfare system, and was easily re-elected in 1996. In terms of foreign policy, Clinton focused on environmental and health concerns, promoting free markets and democracy, and reducing nuclear threats. He also advocated free trade and signed many trade agreements with countries worldwide, including the North American Free Trade Agreement (NAFTA).

Clinton's presidency was tainted, however, by a series of scandals, one of which threatened to remove him from the White House. While Clinton was the governor of Arkansas, he was involved in certain business dealings that were criticized and investigated, though charges were never laid. However, he did face a grand jury investigation as a result of accusations of sexual harassment and impropriety, the most famous of which was the Monica Lewinsky case. Lewinsky was a White House intern with whom the president had engaged in a sexual relationship. At first, Clinton denied the accusations, but as the evidence mounted, he admitted to it and publicly apologized both to Lewinsky and to the American people. Republicans in the House of Representatives moved to have Clinton impeached for obstruction of justice and perjury (lying under oath), but they did not have enough votes in the Senate to convict him, and Clinton remained in office for the rest of his term.

Strangely enough, during the whole Lewinsky scandal, President Clinton's popularity actually increased. Since the 1994 congressional elections, when the Republicans gained a majority of seats, many people felt that the Republicans were more concerned with discrediting Clinton than they were with handling foreign and domestic issues. During the trial, the Republicans were often seen as disagreeable and vindictive. In contrast, Americans generally accepted Clinton's apology and were ready to move on to the real business of the country.

Bill Clinton's first presidential election victory came in part because Americans were gravely concerned about the nation's economy, which had been in a recession for much of George H.W. Bush's presidency.

The United States was also involved in a few military conflicts during the Clinton presidency, mainly under the auspices of a mutual defense alliance called the North Atlantic Treaty Organization (NATO). For example, the U.S. played an active role in Yugoslavia, helping bring an end to violence that had led to numerous atrocities being committed against ethnic minorities in Kosovo. Overall, despite the partisan squabbling and scandals in the White House, most Americans approved of the Clinton presidency and felt that he had been an effective leader.

The presidential election of 2000 matched Texas governor George W. Bush, son of the former president, against Al Gore, Clinton's vice president. It would go down as one of the closest and most contested elections in American history; in fact, it all came down to voters in Florida.

Following accusations of ballot fraud, election officials spent more than a month counting and recounting ballots to determine which candidate had won the state. Finally, with Bush holding onto a very narrow lead, the Supreme Court ruled that the recount process being used was unconstitutional. Bush was declared the winner and was sworn in a month later amid lingering controversy about the fairness of the election.

Chapter 2 discussed the terrorist attack on September 11, 2001, and the War on Terrorism that was launched shortly after. Public support for Bush declined significantly during his second term in office. Toward the end of 2001, Bush had the approval of 88% of the American population, due to the leadership he showed in the days immediately following the 9/11 attacks. In the next several years, however, Bush's approval rating would fall to a low of 27%, owing to negative sentiment concerning the continued struggle in Iraq, the government's perceived mishandling of New Orleans following Hurricane Katrina in 2005, and a variety of unpopular policies enacted by the administration including the Patriot Act, which many saw as a violation of certain civil liberties guaranteed by the U.S. constitution. In addition, during the last few years of Bush's term as president, the country entered an economic downturn which quickly transformed into a global recession, in part due to a lack of regulation of the U.S. banking industry. Although it is too soon to properly assess Bush's place in history, it is clear that the end result of the Iraq War as well as the fallout from the economic downturn will greatly affect how he is remembered.

In 2008, the United States held a critical election. The end of the Iraq War was not in sight, the economy was dangerously unstable, and a growing number of Americans were concerned about losing their homes and jobs, just as the costs of such essentials as health care and energy were rising rapidly. The American people were eager for a change of tune in the federal government, which they found in an unlikely candidate, Senator Barack Obama of Illinois. Campaigning on a message of hope and change, Obama's words inspired millions of Americans who felt that their country was heading down the wrong track. After winning the Democratic Party's nomination over Senator Hillary Rodham Clinton, Obama went on to defeat the Republican candidate, Senator John McCain, in the general election, which boasted the highest voter turnout in the U.S. since the 1960s.

The election of Obama, the first African American to hold the office of President of the United States, was an unprecedented and powerful event for a nation with a long history of racial inequality. During Obama's first days in office, he took steps to repeal some of the more controversial policies that the Bush administration had put in place, and turned his focus toward bringing the U.S. out of economic recession. It was clear that the ideology of the government had changed, and Americans became cautiously hopeful that Obama and the Democratic-majority Congress could set the country on the right track again.

Barack Obama, first African American President of the United States.

Suggested Reading

★ Farber, David, ed. *The 60's: From Memory to History*. Chapel Hill, North Carolina: University of North Carolina Press, 1994.

★ Halberstam, David. *The Fifties*. New York: Ballantine, 1994.

★ Krugman, Paul. *The Return of Depression Economics and the Crisis of 2008*. New York: W. W. Norton, 2008.

★ Obama, Barack. *Change We Can Believe In: Barack Obama's Plan to Renew America's Promise*. New York: Three Rivers Press, 2008.

★ Patterson, James T. Grand Expectations: *The United States, 1945–1974*. New York: Oxford University Press, 1997.

★ Patterson, James T. *Restless Giant: The United States from Watergate to Bush v. Gore*. New York: Oxford University Press, 2007.

★ Schaller, Michael. *Right Turn: American Life in the Reagan–Bush Era, 1980–1992*. New York: Oxford University Press, 2006.

★ Schulman, Bruce. *The Seventies: The Great Shift in American Culture, Society, and Politics*. New York: Da Capo Press, 2002.

★ Whitfield, Stephen J. *The Culture of the Cold War (The American Movement), 2nd ed.* Baltimore, Maryland: The Johns Hopkins University Press, 1996.

Chapter Five • Recap Quiz

1. Which country was the second to develop an atomic bomb?

2. Which U.S. president took a firm stance during the Cuban Missile Crisis?

3. Which president launched the War on Terrorism?

4. What was the name of the scandal that caused President Nixon to resign?

5. Name a cause that President Reagan strongly advocated, and one that he strongly opposed.

6. What nation took dozens of Americans hostage in 1979, damaging President Carter's popularity and chances of being re-elected?

ANSWERS TO QUIZ FIVE

1- Russia   2- John F. Kennedy   3- George W. Bush   4- Watergate

5- advocated tough stance against crime and drugs, opposed abortion

6- Iran

CHAPTER SIX

INFLUENTIAL AMERICANS

While countless individuals have made important contributions to the American way of life and the destiny of the nation, there are those whose legacy will live forever.

THE WHITE HOUSE

The White House, official residence of the President of the U.S., built in its original form between 1792 and 1800, and situated at 1600 Pennsylvania Ave. in Washington, D.C. Known variously through its history as the President's Palace, the President's House, and the Executive Mansion, the building has always been most popularly known as the White House. It has been the home of every president in American history with the exception of George Washington, who approved the act that led to its construction. Although the White House has been subject to numerous renovations and additions, it has retained its classically simple character.

I have a dream that one day this nation will rise up and live out the true meaning of its creed: we hold these truths to be self-evident, that all men are created equal.

MARTIN LUTHER KING
1929–1968

The United States has not grown into the nation it is today through the achievements of only its presidents. There are a great many people who have contributed to the development of the country and who have shaped the American way of life. In chapter 3, we noted that greatness is subjective—a person can be a hero in some people's eyes and a villain in the eyes of others. We suggested that greatness can be measured in terms of the impact that people have and the degree to which they are able to make lasting changes.

The story of America is largely a story of individual courage—people who looked around themselves and saw that things could be better; people who were brave enough to stand up for something new. In almost every case, the heroes of American history have encountered strong opposition; indeed, many have given their lives to their cause. There is often great resistance to change. It can be extremely difficult to get individuals, let alone society as a whole, to change their perspectives. Nonetheless, this is exactly what has happened many times in the history of the United States with regard to such issues as slavery, civil rights, racial tolerance, social responsibility, compassion for the poor, and the willingness to help others around the world.

In this final chapter, we will profile six prominent Americans who have played important roles in the history of the United States. Although it is nearly impossible to pick the "greatest" or "most influential" Americans, we can assess individuals by the ways they are able to affect the world around them. The historical figures selected here represent a cross-section of American society—they are of different races and sexes, and they come from different backgrounds, but they have all made an important contribution to the history of the country. Their stories show that any person with an original and meaningful idea, who is willing to expend a considerable amount of effort, can achieve greatness. It is also important to remember that for everyone who does achieve this distinction, there are millions of others whose names will never be mentioned in any history book, but who have nonetheless made a lasting impact on American life.

MARTIN LUTHER KING, JR. (1929–1968)

Slavery tainted more than 200 years of American history, and following its abolition there were another 100 years of racial prejudice, segregation, and discrimination. Many people simply accepted this as the status quo, resigned to believing that it would always be that way. Dr. Martin Luther King, Jr., a black Baptist minister with a doctorate degree from Boston University, was not one of those people—he believed that change was possible, and he fought for most of his life to achieve equality between the races.

Well into the 1960s, there were many parts of the United States, mainly in the South, that still institutionalized segregation. Blacks were not allowed to attend the same schools, visit the same hospitals, or apply for the same jobs that whites were. There were black restrooms and benches, black sections in movie theaters, black seats on buses. There were clubs and organizations to which blacks could not belong and neighborhoods where it was unsafe for blacks to visit. When the civil rights movement started gaining support, there was considerable anger and resistance to it. Many people believed that blacks and whites could not get along together; some of the more radical groups, such as the Ku Klux Klan, used violent means to resist the growing movement for social change.

Chapter 5 introduced Rosa Parks, who refused to give up her seat on the bus to a white man in Montgomery, Alabama, and Martin Luther King, Jr., who organized a boycott of the Montgomery bus system which eventually led to a federal court ruling that segregation on buses was unconstitutional. During this boycott, King was arrested, his house was bombed, and he and his family were threatened; however, he did not give up his ideal that the United States could become a country for all people, regardless of their race.

Martin Luther King, Jr.
1929–1968

The civil rights movement aimed to do more than change people's attitudes. It sought to change the laws that allowed segregation. The practice of "separate but equal" perpetuated deep social and economic injustices. Civil rights advocates wanted equality in society, in the workforce, and in government.

King believed in nonviolent means of change. He knew that many white Americans were afraid of black people and realized that only by demonstrating how similar the people of each race really were could these barriers of fear be broken down. He used boycotts, marches, demonstrations, and speeches to spread his message. King became recognized as one of the greatest orators in American history. In 1963, he led a march on Washington, D.C., where, standing on the steps of the Lincoln Memorial, he delivered his famous "I have a dream" speech. In that speech, he challenged the country to abolish racism and to live up to the high ideals it had set forth in the Declaration of Independence almost 200 years before:

I have a dream that one day this nation will rise up and live out the true meaning of its creed: "We hold these truths to be self-evident, that all men are created equal."

I have a dream that my four little children will one day live in a nation where they will not be judged by the color of their skin but by the content of their character."

King lived a difficult life. His leadership was challenged by people who did not agree with his methods of nonviolence. Some white people sought to intimidate him, or worse. There were bombings of churches, attacks on civil rights advocates, and counterdemonstrations that were sometimes violent. Through it all, King maintained his composure, his religious convictions, his optimism, and his sense of purpose. In 1964, King became the youngest person ever to receive the Nobel Peace Prize, and he immediately announced that he would donate the money from the prize to the civil rights movement.

Martin Luther King, Jr., was assassinated on April 4, 1968, in Memphis, Tennessee. Although his assassination sparked incidents of violence, the values he devoted his life to fostering prevailed. The civil rights movement gained many new supporters and gradually achieved one success after another, making changes to racist and discriminatory laws on both state and federal levels. In many ways, the civil rights movement is an ongoing struggle and there is still much work to be done. King's legacy lies in showing that equality is necessary in a country that calls itself a democracy, and in his peaceful but forceful approach to achieving that equality.

ALBERT EINSTEIN (1879–1955)

There is more than one way to become an American—some people are born in the United States, others choose to make this country their home. Albert Einstein was born in Germany in 1879. His family moved to Italy and later to Switzerland, where he finished his schooling. He returned to Germany in 1914, but for political reasons (he was a Jew as the Nazis were coming to power), he renounced his German citizenship and

Albert Einstein
1879–1955

immigrated to the United States, becoming an American citizen in 1940. Einstein is known for his contributions to science, which have had many practical applications including in the development of televisions, remote controls, and DVD players, as well as for his pacificism and commitment to social justice. Far beyond the scope of "greatest American," *Time* magazine in 1999 named Einstein the "person of the century"!

Einstein is most famous for his achievements in science, which include his theory of relativity. He worked on quantum theory and sought to unify the laws of physics. He was awarded the Nobel Prize in Physics in 1921. He delivered lectures and taught around the world, finishing off his teaching career as a Professor of Theoretical Physics at Princeton. His work inspired many other scientists around the world and he gained international fame for his theories.

Einstein was also known for being a pacifist. When many of Germany's leading scientists signed a manifesto in support of their country's actions in World War I, Einstein and three others signed an anti-war petition. He served as a political figure in Germany, joining an international committee that was part of the League of Nations, and working actively to promote human rights. He was an outspoken advocate of democracy and critic of fascism. When the Nazi Party started to gain power in Germany, Einstein warned the international community of the threat that Hitler posed (unfortunately, the warnings were not well heeded at the time).

In 1939, Einstein and other physicists realized that the scientific discoveries of the early twentieth century could be used to make weapons unlike any that had been seen before—they could be used to create nuclear bombs. The scientists also had reason to believe that Germany was actively pursuing the development of such weapons. Einstein wrote a letter to President Franklin D. Roosevelt to warn him about the situation and to urge the United States to take action. This letter led the U.S. to launch a project to develop its own nuclear bomb, which was used against Japan to bring an end to World War II. Although Einstein was known as a vocal critic of war in general, he recognized the danger that Hitler and the Nazis presented. There is little doubt that if Germany had developed the bomb first, the outcome of the war would have been vastly different. After the war, Einstein again promoted peace and pacifism, and was a supporter of the United Nations effort at international cooperation; he urged the world never to use the bomb again.

Albert Einstein is regarded as one of the most brilliant and innovative minds of all time. Indeed, his name is synonymous with *genius*. His theories and experiments revolutionized the field of physics and made possible a great many scientific discoveries, of which nuclear weapons were only a small part. His discipline and perseverance, through personal and political difficulties, helped shape him into a well-respected scientific and international figure.

Einstein also worked throughout his life to reconcile science and religion. Unlike many scientists of the day, he believed in God, and he challenged scientists to be open-minded in their pursuits of truth and to assess their discoveries in light of larger truths and values. Throughout his life, he remained an example of integrity and of a willingness to explore truths beyond what he could see.

SUSAN B. ANTHONY (1820–1906)

Many Americans know of Susan B. Anthony as a crusader for the right of American women to vote. Although this is the cause she is most famous for

promoting, Anthony was also an abolitionist, a labor and educational reformer, and an advocate of women's rights in general—a pretty impressive resume for someone who lived in the mid–nineteenth century! Anthony worked her whole life to achieve something that is often taken for granted today: the political equality of women in our society. She was so instrumental to the cause that the Nineteenth Amendment, which gave women the right to vote, is known as the Susan B. Anthony Amendment. Unfortunately, it was not passed until fourteen years after her death.

Born into an activist Quaker family, she grew up in an atmosphere that stressed discipline and principled conviction. After spending many years as a teacher, her first foray into political reform was in the temperance movement which sought to limit the sale of alcohol. In the 1850s, she rallied around the abolitionist movement and after the Civil War became very active in the struggle for women's right to vote, called *suffrage*. She demanded that women be accorded the same rights that were granted to black men at the end of the civil war, leading a vigorous campaign for women's rights that occupied most of the rest of her life.

Anthony lectured across the United States and in Europe. She organized several associations, including the American Equal Rights Association and the American Woman Suffrage Association, and published books and newspapers to promote her cause. In 1872, she led a nonviolent demonstration in Rochester, New York, in which she and several other women were arrested for voting. She gathered petitions and spoke before Congress seeking the right to vote, campaigned for women's right to own property, and gained admittance for women to the University of Rochester. She also worked to promote an eight-hour workday and equal pay for women doing the same work as men. She inspired a great many other women and many men to take up the cause. Starting in Wyoming in 1869, states and territories gradually started extending suffrage to women.

Since Susan B. Anthony, the women's rights movement has continued to grow. Many other American women, along with women in many other parts of the world, have gained recognition for their work for causes such as fair employment practices, equal pay for equal work, and an end to a wide range of economic, social, and political practices that inhibit gender equality.

Anthony's struggle on behalf of American women was similar to King's struggle on behalf of black Americans. Her protests were nonviolent, and she faced powerful opposition which was sometimes violent—yet, in the end, she prevailed. As with the civil rights movement toward racial equality, many feel that there is still much work to be done toward gender equality. Less than a century ago, women earned the right to vote; today, women participate in the

Susan B. Anthony
1820–1906

highest levels of government. Anthony and her contemporaries got the ball rolling, and it has been rolling for about 150 years.

Like Martin Luther King, Jr., and Albert Einstein, Susan B. Anthony's work extended beyond the boundaries of the United States and has influenced the development of the modern world. There are many parts of the world where women continue to be oppressed, but things are gradually changing. The women's rights movement, which largely began in the United States and England, has become a significant international cause and one which has stimulated a great degree of social change in modern society.

CESAR CHAVEZ (1927–1993)

We have seen that several groups have had to struggle to achieve the rights and freedoms that most Americans enjoy today. Those struggles that have shaped the United States have been not only among races or between the sexes, but also among the classes. Working class Americans of all races have struggled to achieve equal protection and fair treatment under the law, and the struggle of organized labor is an important part of American history. Cesar Chavez, a Mexican American, founded America's first farm worker's union. He improved the working conditions of migrant farm workers and to raise awareness about the farming industry. U.S. Senator Robert Kennedy called Chavez "one of the heroic figures of our time."

Chavez was born in Arizona. His family was thrust into poverty after losing their land during the Great Depression, and he had to leave school to help support his family, who became migrant workers—they traveled from place to place, farming whatever crops were in season. He served in the U.S. Navy during the end of World War II. He had served his country and put his life on the line, and he felt that as a farm worker he should be

Cesar Chavez
1927–1993

treated as well as any other laborer. Like the other people we have seen in this chapter, Chavez knew that he could help improve the situation.

In the 1950s, Chavez started working with the Community Service Organization, which fought against racial and economic discrimination against Mexican Americans. In the early 1960s, he turned his attention toward farm workers, who had been excluded from many labor unions at the time, and founded an organization which later became the United Farm Workers Union (UFW). Like Susan B. Anthony and Martin Luther King, Jr., Chavez used nonviolent methods, including hunger strikes, to promote his cause. In 1965, he rose to national and international fame when he led a strike and boycott of table and wine grapes. The working conditions for farmers, especially migrant workers, at the time were deplorable—they were paid a meager wage and were often exposed to harsh chemicals and pesticides. As the American public became more educated about these conditions, more pressure was placed on grape growers. The strike–boycott was so effective that by 1970, many of the major grape growers had signed contracts with Chavez's organization. These contracts guaranteed workers higher pay as well as health and pension benefits. The UFW also led boycotts of lettuce to improve working conditions, and later led more grape boycotts to raise awareness about the use of pesticides.

The contributions of Cesar Chavez to the farm workers movement stand alongside those of many other people who worked to improve pay and conditions for laborers in factories, coal mines, shipyards, and virtually every other part of American industry. As with the struggles for civil and women's rights, there was initially considerable and powerful opposition to the labor movement—in its early days, unions were seen as being equated with communism and their leaders disparaged as traitors to America. Although most labor leaders organized legal strikes and peaceful demonstrations, some business owners used violent tactics to break up and suppress the movement. It took a long time and a gradual education of the American public before some politicians were convinced to support labor unions. Today, American labor law is much more effective

at protecting worker's rights, and Cesar Chavez is one of the many dedicated people that the American worker has to thank.

SITTING BULL (1831?–1890)

At first glance, it may seem strange to include Sitting Bull in a list of great Americans, particularly since at the time he lived he would not have been considered an "American" at all. We have seen that many groups have had to struggle to achieve the rights and freedoms guaranteed to all Americans. We have been discussing greatness mainly in terms of success stories; however, there are great men and women who fought valiantly for their cause and were eventually defeated. These defeats have contributed as much to the fabric of American society as the successes we have described. Even in people who have suffered defeat, we can recognize the qualities of integrity, dedication, and inspiration that we value so highly. Throughout much of his life, Sioux chief Sitting Bull was feared and despised by white Americans. Today, however, we can look at him with admiration for standing up to oppression and for fighting to preserve the way of life of his people.

Sitting Bull was born around 1831 into the Hunkpapa Sioux tribe in what is now South Dakota. He became part of the Strong Heart warrior society and worked to ensure tribal welfare. His first scrimmage

Sitting Bull
1831?–1890

with white soldiers occurred in 1863, and much of the rest of his life was dedicated to military campaigns. He was responsible for some of the most stunning Native American victories in the Indian Wars. He became the chief of the Sioux nation in 1868.

Although much of his fame comes from his bravery in armed campaigns, Sitting Bull also used nonviolent methods of protest. Foreshadowing the "sit-ins" that were part of the civil rights movement, Sitting Bull is said once to have led his warriors to the middle of a battlefield and calmly smoked a peace pipe.

In the 1870s, gold was discovered in a region of Dakota Territory that had been given to the American Indians in a treaty just a few years earlier. The government tried to buy back the land, and when those efforts failed, they decided to just take it. Sitting Bull and his people refused to leave their land for the reservation and were considered hostile to the U.S. government. This conflict led to the Battle of Little Bighorn in which Sioux warriors decimated the forces of U.S. lieutenant colonel George Custer. The U.S. military sent more forces to drive the Indians back, and many were forced to surrender. In 1877, Sitting Bull led his tribe into Canada; however, a few years later famine forced them to return to the United States and surrender. Throughout the rest of his life, he was still considered a threat to white Americans and he was killed in 1890 as his followers tried to protect him from policemen who were trying to arrest him.

Sitting Bull was admired and respected by Native Americans, not only for his military successes but also as a loving father of his people. He understood that the Indian way of life was dependent on the freedom to use ancestral land, and his tribe needed to be able to hunt buffalo to survive. He watched as white men repeatedly violated treaties, appropriated resources, and killed the buffalo almost to extinction. Some of the laws made by the U.S. government would have been impossible for Sitting Bull to obey even if he had wanted to. For example, all Sioux were ordered to settle on reservations by a specified date in 1876 or they would be considered hostile to the United States. It would not have been possible for Sitting Bull to move his entire tribe the required distance in the winter, so he had no choice but to refuse.

Sitting Bull's life is not a great American success story. However, even though he did not achieve his desired objectives, his influence was pervasive among native peoples of America and beyond. As tolerance grew and American Indians started to be seen in a less harsh light, the public began to view Sitting Bull's story from a new perspective. To this day, Native Americans have not been able to achieve the social and economic equality that so many groups have struggled for. Even into the 1950s, most American children studied history books that characterized American Indians as ruthless and savage people. Today, most people can look on the events of the past with a better understanding of the struggles that they faced when white Americans began to occupy larger and larger regions of the country. As the social conscience of the American public continues to evolve, there is now a greater appreciation of the cultures, values, and beliefs of the "original" Americans.

JOHN GLENN (1921–)

John Glenn is a little different than the other people that have been profiled in this chapter. He is not particularly known for advancing a specific cause in the face of violent opposition. Rather, his entire life serves as an example of heroism and many of the qualities that are valued by Americans. He has contributed to several aspects of both public and private life.

Glenn joined the U.S. Marine Corps in 1943 and served as fighter pilot in both World War II and the Korean War. He was highly decorated for this service, receiving the Distinguished Flying Cross six times. He then spent time as a test pilot, and in 1957 he set a transcontinental speed record by traveling from Los Angeles to New York in three hours and twenty-three minutes. He was selected as one of the first people to be involved in the Mercury Space Program and was the third American in space. In 1962, he piloted the *Friendship 7* spacecraft in the first manned mission to successfully orbit the earth. This mission was seen as a great success for the American space program, which at the time was involved in a "space race" with the Soviet Union.

Thirty-six years later, in October of 1998, Glenn was selected to become the world's oldest man in space and returned to his role of astronaut aboard the space shuttle *Discovery*. In the intervening years, he led an active political life and even ran for President of the United States in 1984.

Glenn was seventy-seven when he served as a crew member on the *Discovery*. Given the intense physical demands of space travel, there were many who wondered if he could withstand the stress. Even as an original member of the Mercury program, he was older than the other astronauts—he was already forty when he made his historic flight in 1962.

John Glenn
1921–

In 1974, Glenn was elected to the U.S. Senate. He was an author of the 1978 Nuclear Nonproliferation Act, which sought to limit the spread of nuclear weapons, and sat on the Foreign Relations and Armed Services committees and the Special Committee on Aging. He was respected by members of both political parties as being honest and reliable.

On a few occasions, Glenn came close to losing his life. In one combat flight over Korea, his aircraft was hit with heavy antiaircraft fire that punctured his plane with more than 200 bullet and shrapnel holes. He barely managed to keep it from crashing. Even his 1962 space flight flirted with disaster. During re-entry into the earth's atmosphere, there was a problem with the heat shield and many of the NASA launch control personnel feared that he and his capsule would burn up before he managed to land in the ocean.

Afterward, he was prevented from returning to space, partly because of his age, yet the man who seemed a little too old to travel to space in 1964 proved to be up to the task in 1998!

John Glenn is not only a decorated war hero and respected American politician; he is an example of exceptional personal character. As a politician, he showed that nice guys don't always finish last.

The United States owes its achievements to the many great men and women who have struggled to improve the lives of those around them. Many of these struggles have happened out of the public eye. While it is easy to look to heroes, the greatness of the nation lies equally in ordinary hard-working Americans who do their jobs to the best of their ability, put their lives on the line when necessary, and keep the country moving in a positive direction for all members of society.

Suggested Reading

★ Glenn, John and Nick Taylor. *John Glenn: A Memoir*. New York: Bantam Dell, 2000.

★ Hansen, Drew. *The Dream: Martin Luther King, Jr., and the Speech that Inspired a Nation*. New York: Harper Perennial, 2005.

★ Isaacson, Walter. *Einstein: His Life and Universe*. New York: Simon & Schuster, 2008.

★ Levy, Jacques E. and Barbara Moulton. *Cesar Chavez: Autobiography of La Causa*. Minneapolis, Minnesota: University of Minnesota Press, 2007.

★ Sherr, Lynn. *Failure Is Impossible: Susan B. Anthony in Her Own Words*. New York: Three Rivers Press, 1996.

★ Utley, Robert M. *Sitting Bull: The Life and Times of an American Patriot*. New York: Henry Holt and Company, 1993.

1. Who won the Nobel Peace Prize in 1964?

2. Which president did Albert Einstein convince to start work on an atomic bomb?

3. Susan B. Anthony fought for the right of American women to vote, but died fourteen years before this right became the subject of a Constitutional amendment. In what year did she die?

4. What was the name of the famous battle in which Sitting Bull defeated Lieutenant Colonel George Custer?

5. What was the name of the space capsule in which John Glenn became the first man to orbit the earth?

6. In the late 1960s, Cesar Chavez successfully led a strike-boycott of what agricultural product?

ANSWERS TO QUIZ SIX

1- Martin Luther King, Jr.   2- Franklin D. Roosevelt   3- 1906

4- the Battle of Little Bighorn   5- Friendship 7   6- grapes

Appendix A • Chronology

The following is an abbreviated listing of many important events in American history, showing their dates and the order in which they occurred. It includes events discussed in this text, as well as others which were not mentioned here, but which you may wish to investigate through further reading.

★ ≈ 13,500 B.C. — Paleo-Indians cross land bridge from Siberia to North America

★ 1492 — Christopher Columbus lands in the New World

★ 1607 — First British colony settled at Jamestown, Virginia

★ 1619 — First Africans arrive in New World on Dutch slave ship

★ 1620 — Pilgrims land at Plymouth, Massachusetts

★ 1754 — French and Indian War begins

★ 1763 — French and Indian War ends; Proclamation of 1763

★ 1764 — Sugar Act

★ 1765 — Quartering Act; Stamp Act

★ 1766 — Declaratory Act

★ 1767 — Start of Townshend Acts

★ 1773 — Tea Act; Boston Tea Party

★ 1774 — Coercive (Intolerable) Acts; First Continental Congress

★ 1775 — Revolutionary War begins

★ 1776 — Second Continental Congress; Thomas Jefferson and others write the Declaration of Independence

★ 1783 — Revolutionary War ends

★ 1787 — Founding Fathers write the Constitution

★ 1789 — George Washington becomes president

★ 1791 — Bill of Rights ratified

★ 1797 — John Adams becomes president

★ 1801 — Thomas Jefferson becomes president

★ 1803 — Louisiana Purchase

★ 1808 — Congress prohibits importation of slaves

★ 1809 — James Madison becomes president

★ 1812 — War of 1812 begins

★ 1815 — War of 1812 ends

★ 1817 — James Monroe becomes president

★ 1820 — Missouri Compromise

★ 1825 — John Quincy Adams becomes president

★ 1829 — Andrew Jackson becomes president

★ 1830 — Indian Removal Act

★ 1837 — Martin Van Buren becomes president

★ 1838 — Cherokee "Trail of Tears"

★ 1841 — William Henry Harrison becomes president, dies of pneumonia; John Tyler becomes president

★ 1845 — James K. Polk becomes president

★ 1846 — Mexican–American War begins

★ 1848 — Mexican–American War ends; gold discovered in California

★ 1849 — Zachary Taylor becomes president

★ 1850 — Millard Fillmore becomes president

★ 1853 — Franklin Pierce becomes president

★ 1854 — Kansas–Nebraska Act

★ 1857 — James Buchanan becomes president

★ 1858 — Lincoln–Douglas debates

★ 1861 — Abraham Lincoln becomes president; Civil War begins

★ 1863 — Emancipation Proclamation

★ 1865 — Civil War ends; Abraham Lincoln assassinated; Andrew Johnson becomes president; slavery outlawed

★ 1867 — Reconstruction Acts

★ 1869 — Ulysses S. Grant becomes president

★ 1876 — Battle of Little Bighorn

★ 1877 — Rutherford B. Hayes becomes president

★ 1881 — James Garfield becomes president, assassinated; Chester A. Arthur becomes president

★ 1885 — Grover Cleveland becomes president

★ 1889 — Benjamin Harrison becomes president

★ 1890 — Wounded Knee Massacre

★ 1893 — Grover Cleveland becomes president

★ 1897 — William McKinley becomes president

★ 1898 — Spanish–American War; United States annexes Hawaii

★ 1901 — William McKinley assassinated; Theodore Roosevelt becomes president

★ 1909 — William Howard Taft becomes president

★ 1913 — Woodrow Wilson becomes president

★ 1914 — World War I begins

★ 1915 — Sinking of Lusitania

★ 1917 — United States enters World War I; Selective Service Act

★ 1918 — Germany requests armistice

★ 1919 — World War I peace treaty signed

★ 1920 — Women granted right to vote

★ 1921 — Warren G. Harding becomes president

★ 1923 — Warren G. Harding dies of a heart attack; Calvin Coolidge becomes president

★ 1929 — Herbert Hoover becomes president; stock market crashes leading to the Great Depression

★ 1933 — Franklin D. Roosevelt becomes president, begins New Deal reforms; Nazi Party elected in Germany

★ 1935 — Social Security Act

★ 1939 — World War II begins

★ 1941 — Japan attacks Pearl Harbor; United States enters World War II

★ 1944 — D-Day attacks

★ 1945 — Franklin D. Roosevelt dies of cerebral hemorrhage; Harry S. Truman becomes president; United States uses atomic bombs on Hiroshima and Nagasaki; World War II ends; United Nations established; Cold War begins

★ 1947 — Truman Doctrine

★ 1948 — Marshall Plan

★ 1950 — Korean War begins

★ 1953 — Dwight D. Eisenhower becomes president; Korean War ends

★ 1955 — Rosa Parks refuses to give up seat on bus; Montgomery bus boycott; segregation of schools outlawed

★ 1959 — Alaska, Hawaii become last two states admitted to Union

★ 1961 — John F. Kennedy becomes president; Bay of Pigs invasion

★ 1962 — Cuban missile crisis

★ 1963 — John F. Kennedy assassinated; Lyndon B. Johnson becomes president; Martin Luther King, Jr. delivers "I have a dream" speech

★ 1964 — Gulf of Tonkin sparks major U.S. involvement in Vietnam War; Civil Rights Act outlaws segregation

★ 1968 — Martin Luther King, Jr., assassinated

★ 1969 — Richard M. Nixon becomes president; Neil Armstrong becomes first man on the moon

★ 1973 — United States signs peace accord with North Korea

★ 1974 — Richard M. Nixon resigns; Gerald R. Ford becomes president

★ 1975 — Vietnam War ends

★ 1977 — James Carter becomes president

★ 1979 — Americans taken hostage in Iran

★ 1981 — Ronald Reagan becomes president

★ 1989 — George H.W. Bush becomes president; Soviet Union collapses; Cold War ends

★ 1990 — Iraq invades Kuwait; Persian Gulf War begins

★ 1991 — Persian Gulf War ends

★ 1993 — William J. Clinton becomes president

★ 2001 — George W. Bush becomes president; 9/11 attacks; War in Afghanistan begins

★ 2003 — Iraq War begins; George W. Bush declares end of major combat

★ 2005 — Hurricane Katrina

★ 2006 — Saddam Hussein executed

★ 2007 — United States enters economic recession

★ 2009 — Barack Obama becomes president

Appendix B • The Declaration of Independence

★

Complete Text – Transcription

IN CONGRESS, July 4, 1776.

The unanimous Declaration of the thirteen united States of America,

When in the Course of human events, it becomes necessary for one people to dissolve the political bands which have connected them with another, and to assume among the powers of the earth, the separate and equal station to which the Laws of Nature and of Nature's God entitle them, a decent respect to the opinions of mankind requires that they should declare the causes which impel them to the separation.

We hold these truths to be self-evident, that all men are created equal, that they are endowed by their Creator with certain unalienable Rights, that among these are Life, Liberty and the pursuit of Happiness. — That to secure these rights, Governments are instituted among Men, deriving their just powers from the consent of the governed, — That whenever any Form of Government becomes destructive of these ends, it is the Right of the People to alter or to abolish it, and to institute new Government, laying its foundation on such principles and organizing its powers in such form, as to them shall seem most likely to effect their Safety and Happiness. Prudence, indeed, will dictate that Governments long established should not be changed for light and transient causes; and accordingly all experience hath shewn, that mankind are more disposed to suffer, while evils are sufferable, than to right themselves by abolishing the forms to which they are accustomed. But when a long train of abuses and usurpations, pursuing invariably the same Object evinces a design to reduce them under absolute Despotism, it is their right, it is their duty, to throw off such Government, and to provide new Guards for their future security. — Such has been the patient sufferance of these Colonies; and such is now the necessity which constrains them to alter their former Systems of Government. The history of the present King of Great Britain is a history of repeated injuries and usurpations, all having in direct object the establishment of an absolute Tyranny over these States. To prove this, let Facts be submitted to a candid world.

He has refused his Assent to Laws, the most wholesome and necessary for the public good.

He has forbidden his Governors to pass Laws of immediate and pressing importance, unless suspended in their operation till his Assent should be obtained; and when so suspended, he has utterly neglected to attend to them.

He has refused to pass other Laws for the accommodation of large districts of people, unless those people would relinquish the right of Representation in the Legislature, a right inestimable to them and formidable to tyrants only.

He has called together legislative bodies at places unusual, uncomfortable, and distant from the depository of their public Records, for the sole purpose of fatiguing them into compliance with his measures.

He has dissolved Representative Houses repeatedly, for opposing with manly firmness his invasions on the rights of the people.

He has refused for a long time, after such dissolutions, to cause others to be elected; whereby the Legislative powers, incapable of Annihilation, have returned to the People at large for their exercise; the State remaining in the mean time exposed to all the dangers of invasion from without, and convulsions within.

He has endeavoured to prevent the population of these States; for that purpose obstructing the Laws for Naturalization of Foreigners; refusing to pass others to encourage their migrations hither, and raising the conditions of new Appropriations of Lands.

He has obstructed the Administration of Justice, by refusing his Assent to Laws for establishing Judiciary powers.

He has made Judges dependent on his Will alone, for the tenure of their offices, and the amount and payment of their salaries.

He has erected a multitude of New Offices, and sent hither swarms of Officers to harrass our people, and eat out their substance.

He has kept among us, in times of peace, Standing Armies without the Consent of our legislatures.

He has affected to render the Military independent of and superior to the Civil power.

He has combined with others to subject us to a jurisdiction foreign to our constitution, and unacknowledged by our laws; giving his Assent to their Acts of pretended Legislation:

For Quartering large bodies of armed troops among us:

For protecting them, by a mock Trial, from punishment for any Murders which they should commit on the Inhabitants of these States:

For cutting off our Trade with all parts of the world:

For imposing Taxes on us without our Consent:

For depriving us, in many cases, of the benefits of Trial by Jury:

For transporting us beyond Seas to be tried for pretended offences:

For abolishing the free System of English Laws in a neighbouring Province, establishing therein an Arbitrary government, and enlarging its Boundaries so as to render it at once an example and fit instrument for introducing the same absolute rule into these Colonies:

For taking away our Charters, abolishing our most valuable Laws, and altering fundamentally the Forms of our Governments:

For suspending our own Legislatures, and declaring themselves invested with power to legislate for us in all cases whatsoever.

He has abdicated Government here, by declaring us out of his Protection and waging War against us.

He has plundered our seas, ravaged our Coasts, burnt our towns, and destroyed the lives of our people.

He is at this time transporting large Armies of foreign Mercenaries to compleat the works of death, desolation and tyranny, already begun with circumstances of Cruelty & perfidy scarcely paralleled in the most barbarous ages, and totally unworthy the Head of a civilized nation.

He has constrained our fellow Citizens taken Captive on the high Seas to bear Arms against their Country, to become the executioners of their friends and Brethren, or to fall themselves by their Hands.

He has excited domestic insurrections amongst us, and has endeavoured to bring on the inhabitants of our frontiers, the merciless Indian Savages, whose known rule of warfare, is an undistinguished destruction of all ages, sexes and conditions.

In every stage of these Oppressions We have Petitioned for Redress in the most humble terms: Our repeated Petitions have been answered only by repeated injury. A Prince whose character is thus marked by every act which may define a Tyrant, is unfit to be the ruler of a free people.

Nor have We been wanting in attentions to our Brittish brethren. We have warned them from time to time of attempts by their legislature to extend an unwarrantable jurisdiction over us. We have reminded them of the circumstances of our emigration and settlement here. We have appealed to their native justice and magnanimity, and we have conjured them by the ties of our common kindred to disavow these usurpations, which, would inevitably interrupt our connections and correspondence. They too have been deaf to the voice of justice and of consanguinity. We must, therefore, acquiesce in the necessity, which denounces our Separation, and hold them, as we hold the rest of mankind, Enemies in War, in Peace Friends.

We, therefore, the Representatives of the united States of America, in General Congress, Assembled, appealing to the Supreme Judge of the world for the rectitude of our intentions, do, in the Name, and by Authority of the good People of these Colonies, solemnly publish and declare, That these United Colonies are, and of Right ought to be Free and Independent States; that they are Absolved from all Allegiance to the British Crown, and that all political connection between them and the State of Great Britain, is and ought to be totally dissolved; and that as Free and Independent States, they have full Power to levy War, conclude Peace, contract Alliances, establish Commerce, and to do all other Acts and Things which Independent States may of right do. And for the support of this Declaration, with a firm reliance on the protection of divine Providence, we mutually pledge to each other our Lives, our Fortunes and our sacred Honor.

Complete Text – Transcription

Constitution of the United States of America

We the People of the United States, in Order to form a more perfect Union, establish Justice, insure domestic Tranquility, provide for the common defense, promote the general Welfare, and secure the Blessings of Liberty to ourselves and our Posterity, do ordain and establish this Constitution for the United States of America.

Section. 1.

All legislative Powers herein granted shall be vested in a Congress of the United States, which shall consist of a Senate and House of Representatives.

Section. 2.

The House of Representatives shall be composed of Members chosen every second Year by the People of the several States, and the Electors in each State shall have the Qualifications requisite for Electors of the most numerous Branch of the State Legislature.

No Person shall be a Representative who shall not have attained to the Age of twenty five Years, and been seven Years a Citizen of the United States, and who shall not, when elected, be an Inhabitant of that State in which he shall be chosen.

Representatives and direct Taxes shall be apportioned among the several States which may be included within this Union, according to their respective Numbers, which shall be determined by adding to the whole Number of free Persons, including those bound to Service for a Term of Years, and excluding Indians not taxed, three fifths of all other Persons. The actual Enumeration shall be made within three Years after the first Meeting of the Congress of the United States, and within every subsequent Term of ten Years, in such Manner as they shall by Law direct. The Number of Representatives shall not exceed one for every thirty Thousand, but each State shall have at Least one Representative; and until such enumeration shall be made, the State of New Hampshire shall be entitled to chuse three, Massachusetts eight, Rhode-Island and Providence

Plantations one, Connecticut five, New-York six, New Jersey four, Pennsylvania eight, Delaware one, Maryland six, Virginia ten, North Carolina five, South Carolina five, and Georgia three.

When vacancies happen in the Representation from any State, the Executive Authority thereof shall issue Writs of Election to fill such Vacancies.

The House of Representatives shall chuse their Speaker and other Officers; and shall have the sole Power of Impeachment.

Section. 3.

The Senate of the United States shall be composed of two Senators from each State, chosen by the Legislature thereof for six Years; and each Senator shall have one Vote.

Immediately after they shall be assembled in Consequence of the first Election, they shall be divided as equally as may be into three Classes. The Seats of the Senators of the first Class shall be vacated at the Expiration of the second Year, of the second Class at the Expiration of the fourth Year, and of the third Class at the Expiration of the sixth Year, so that one third may be chosen every second Year; and if Vacancies happen by Resignation, or otherwise, during the Recess of the Legislature of any State, the Executive thereof may make temporary Appointments until the next Meeting of the Legislature, which shall then fill such Vacancies.

No Person shall be a Senator who shall not have attained to the Age of thirty Years, and been nine Years a Citizen of the United States, and who shall not, when elected, be an Inhabitant of that State for which he shall be chosen.

The Vice President of the United States shall be President of the Senate, but shall have no Vote, unless they be equally divided.

The Senate shall chuse their other Officers, and also a President pro tempore, in the Absence of the Vice President, or when he shall exercise the Office of President of the United States.

The Senate shall have the sole Power to try all Impeachments. When sitting for that Purpose, they shall be on Oath or Affirmation. When the President of the United States is tried, the Chief Justice shall preside: And no Person shall be convicted without the Concurrence of two thirds of the Members present.

Judgment in Cases of Impeachment shall not extend further than to removal from Office, and disqualification to hold and enjoy any Office of honor, Trust or Profit under the

United States: but the Party convicted shall nevertheless be liable and subject to Indictment, Trial, Judgment and Punishment, according to Law.

Section. 4.

The Times, Places and Manner of holding Elections for Senators and Representatives, shall be prescribed in each State by the Legislature thereof; but the Congress may at any time by Law make or alter such Regulations, except as to the Places of chusing Senators.

The Congress shall assemble at least once in every Year, and such Meeting shall be on the first Monday in December, unless they shall by Law appoint a different Day.

Section. 5.

Each House shall be the Judge of the Elections, Returns and Qualifications of its own Members, and a Majority of each shall constitute a Quorum to do Business; but a smaller Number may adjourn from day to day, and may be authorized to compel the Attendance of absent Members, in such Manner, and under such Penalties as each House may provide.

Each House may determine the Rules of its Proceedings, punish its Members for disorderly Behaviour, and, with the Concurrence of two thirds, expel a Member.

Each House shall keep a Journal of its Proceedings, and from time to time publish the same, excepting such Parts as may in their Judgment require Secrecy; and the Yeas and Nays of the Members of either House on any question shall, at the Desire of one fifth of those Present, be entered on the Journal.

Neither House, during the Session of Congress, shall, without the Consent of the other, adjourn for more than three days, nor to any other Place than that in which the two Houses shall be sitting.

Section. 6.

The Senators and Representatives shall receive a Compensation for their Services, to be ascertained by Law, and paid out of the Treasury of the United States. They shall in all Cases, except Treason, Felony and Breach of the Peace, be privileged from Arrest during their Attendance at the Session of their respective Houses, and in going to and returning from the same; and for any Speech or Debate in either House, they shall not be questioned in any other Place.

No Senator or Representative shall, during the Time for which he was elected, be appointed to any civil Office under the Authority of the United States, which shall have been created, or the Emoluments whereof shall have been encreased during such time; and no Person holding any Office under the United States, shall be a Member of either House during his Continuance in Office.

Section. 7.

All Bills for raising Revenue shall originate in the House of Representatives; but the Senate may propose or concur with Amendments as on other Bills.

Every Bill which shall have passed the House of Representatives and the Senate, shall, before it become a Law, be presented to the President of the United States: If he approve he shall sign it, but if not he shall return it, with his Objections to that House in which it shall have originated, who shall enter the Objections at large on their Journal, and proceed to reconsider it. If after such Reconsideration two thirds of that House shall agree to pass the Bill, it shall be sent, together with the Objections, to the other House, by which it shall likewise be reconsidered, and if approved by two thirds of that House, it shall become a Law. But in all such Cases the Votes of both Houses shall be determined by yeas and Nays, and the Names of the Persons voting for and against the Bill shall be entered on the Journal of each House respectively. If any Bill shall not be returned by the President within ten Days (Sundays excepted) after it shall have been presented to him, the Same shall be a Law, in like Manner as if he had signed it, unless the Congress by their Adjournment prevent its Return, in which Case it shall not be a Law.

Every Order, Resolution, or Vote to which the Concurrence of the Senate and House of Representatives may be necessary (except on a question of Adjournment) shall be presented to the President of the United States; and before the Same shall take Effect, shall be approved by him, or being disapproved by him, shall be repassed by two thirds of the Senate and House of Representatives, according to the Rules and Limitations prescribed in the Case of a Bill.

Section. 8.

The Congress shall have Power To lay and collect Taxes, Duties, Imposts and Excises, to pay the Debts and provide for the common Defence and general Welfare of the United States; but all Duties, Imposts and Excises shall be uniform throughout the United States;

To borrow Money on the credit of the United States;

To regulate Commerce with foreign Nations, and among the several States, and with the Indian Tribes;

To establish an uniform Rule of Naturalization, and uniform Laws on the subject of Bankruptcies throughout the United States;

To coin Money, regulate the Value thereof, and of foreign Coin, and fix the Standard of Weights and Measures;

To provide for the Punishment of counterfeiting the Securities and current Coin of the United States;

To establish Post Offices and post Roads;

To promote the Progress of Science and useful Arts, by securing for limited Times to Authors and Inventors the exclusive Right to their respective Writings and Discoveries;

To constitute Tribunals inferior to the supreme Court;

To define and punish Piracies and Felonies committed on the high Seas, and Offences against the Law of Nations;

To declare War, grant Letters of Marque and Reprisal, and make Rules concerning Captures on Land and Water;

To raise and support Armies, but no Appropriation of Money to that Use shall be for a longer Term than two Years;

To provide and maintain a Navy;

To make Rules for the Government and Regulation of the land and naval Forces;

To provide for calling forth the Militia to execute the Laws of the Union, suppress Insurrections and repel Invasions;

To provide for organizing, arming, and disciplining, the Militia, and for governing such Part of them as may be employed in the Service of the United States, reserving to the States respectively, the Appointment of the Officers, and the Authority of training the Militia according to the discipline prescribed by Congress;

To exercise exclusive Legislation in all Cases whatsoever, over such District (not exceeding ten Miles square) as may, by Cession of particular States, and the Acceptance of Congress, become the Seat of the Government of the United States, and to exercise like Authority over all Places purchased by the Consent of the Legislature of the State in which the Same shall be, for the Erection of Forts, Magazines, Arsenals, dock-Yards, and other needful Buildings;—And

To make all Laws which shall be necessary and proper for carrying into Execution the foregoing Powers, and all other Powers vested by this Constitution in the Government of the United States, or in any Department or Officer thereof.

Section. 9.

The Migration or Importation of such Persons as any of the States now existing shall think proper to admit, shall not be prohibited by the Congress prior to the Year one thousand eight hundred and eight, but a Tax or duty may be imposed on such Importation, not exceeding ten dollars for each Person.

The Privilege of the Writ of Habeas Corpus shall not be suspended, unless when in Cases of Rebellion or Invasion the public Safety may require it.

No Bill of Attainder or ex post facto Law shall be passed.

No Capitation, or other direct, Tax shall be laid, unless in Proportion to the Census or enumeration herein before directed to be taken.

No Tax or Duty shall be laid on Articles exported from any State.

No Preference shall be given by any Regulation of Commerce or Revenue to the Ports of one State over those of another; nor shall Vessels bound to, or from, one State, be obliged to enter, clear, or pay Duties in another.

No Money shall be drawn from the Treasury, but in Consequence of Appropriations made by Law; and a regular Statement and Account of the Receipts and Expenditures of all public Money shall be published from time to time.

No Title of Nobility shall be granted by the United States: And no Person holding any Office of Profit or Trust under them, shall, without the Consent of the Congress, accept of any present, Emolument, Office, or Title, of any kind whatever, from any King, Prince, or foreign State.

Section. 10.

No State shall enter into any Treaty, Alliance, or Confederation; grant Letters of Marque and Reprisal; coin Money; emit Bills of Credit; make any Thing but gold and silver Coin a Tender in Payment of Debts; pass any Bill of Attainder, ex post facto Law, or Law impairing the Obligation of Contracts, or grant any Title of Nobility.

No State shall, without the Consent of the Congress, lay any Imposts or Duties on Imports or Exports, except what may be absolutely necessary for executing it's inspection

Laws: and the net Produce of all Duties and Imposts, laid by any State on Imports or Exports, shall be for the Use of the Treasury of the United States; and all such Laws shall be subject to the Revision and Controul of the Congress.

No State shall, without the Consent of Congress, lay any Duty of Tonnage, keep Troops, or Ships of War in time of Peace, enter into any Agreement or Compact with another State, or with a foreign Power, or engage in War, unless actually invaded, or in such imminent Danger as will not admit of delay.

Article. II.

Section. 1.

The executive Power shall be vested in a President of the United States of America. He shall hold his Office during the Term of four Years, and, together with the Vice President, chosen for the same Term, be elected, as follows:

Each State shall appoint, in such Manner as the Legislature thereof may direct, a Number of Electors, equal to the whole Number of Senators and Representatives to which the State may be entitled in the Congress: but no Senator or Representative, or Person holding an Office of Trust or Profit under the United States, shall be appointed an Elector.

The Electors shall meet in their respective States, and vote by Ballot for two Persons, of whom one at least shall not be an Inhabitant of the same State with themselves. And they shall make a List of all the Persons voted for, and of the Number of Votes for each; which List they shall sign and certify, and transmit sealed to the Seat of the Government of the United States, directed to the President of the Senate. The President of the Senate shall, in the Presence of the Senate and House of Representatives, open all the Certificates, and the Votes shall then be counted. The Person having the greatest Number of Votes shall be the President, if such Number be a Majority of the whole Number of Electors appointed; and if there be more than one who have such Majority, and have an equal Number of Votes, then the House of Representatives shall immediately chuse by Ballot one of them for President; and if no Person have a Majority, then from the five highest on the List the said House shall in like Manner chuse the President. But in chusing the President, the Votes shall be taken by States, the Representation from each State having one Vote; A quorum for this purpose shall consist of a Member or Members from two thirds of the States, and a Majority of all the States shall be necessary to a Choice. In every Case, after the Choice of the President, the Person having the greatest Number of Votes of the Electors shall be the Vice President. But if there should remain two or more who have equal Votes, the Senate shall chuse from them by Ballot the Vice President.

The Congress may determine the Time of chusing the Electors, and the Day on which they shall give their Votes; which Day shall be the same throughout the United States.

No Person except a natural born Citizen, or a Citizen of the United States, at the time of the Adoption of this Constitution, shall be eligible to the Office of President; neither shall any Person be eligible to that Office who shall not have attained to the Age of thirty five Years, and been fourteen Years a Resident within the United States.

In Case of the Removal of the President from Office, or of his Death, Resignation, or Inability to discharge the Powers and Duties of the said Office, the Same shall devolve on the Vice President, and the Congress may by Law provide for the Case of Removal, Death, Resignation or Inability, both of the President and Vice President, declaring what Officer shall then act as President, and such Officer shall act accordingly, until the Disability be removed, or a President shall be elected.

The President shall, at stated Times, receive for his Services, a Compensation, which shall neither be increased nor diminished during the Period for which he shall have been elected, and he shall not receive within that Period any other Emolument from the United States, or any of them.

Before he enter on the Execution of his Office, he shall take the following Oath or Affirmation:—"I do solemnly swear (or affirm) that I will faithfully execute the Office of President of the United States, and will to the best of my Ability, preserve, protect and defend the Constitution of the United States."

Section. 2.

The President shall be Commander in Chief of the Army and Navy of the United States, and of the Militia of the several States, when called into the actual Service of the United States; he may require the Opinion, in writing, of the principal Officer in each of the executive Departments, upon any Subject relating to the Duties of their respective Offices, and he shall have Power to grant Reprieves and Pardons for Offences against the United States, except in Cases of Impeachment.

He shall have Power, by and with the Advice and Consent of the Senate, to make Treaties, provided two thirds of the Senators present concur; and he shall nominate, and by and with the Advice and Consent of the Senate, shall appoint Ambassadors, other public Ministers and Consuls, Judges of the supreme Court, and all other Officers of the United States, whose Appointments are not herein otherwise provided for, and which shall be established by Law: but the Congress may by Law vest the Appointment of such inferior Officers, as they think proper, in the President alone, in the Courts of Law, or in the Heads of Departments.

The President shall have Power to fill up all Vacancies that may happen during the Recess of the Senate, by granting Commissions which shall expire at the End of their next Session.

Section. 3.

He shall from time to time give to the Congress Information of the State of the Union, and recommend to their Consideration such Measures as he shall judge necessary and expedient; he may, on extraordinary Occasions, convene both Houses, or either of them, and in Case of Disagreement between them, with Respect to the Time of Adjournment, he may adjourn them to such Time as he shall think proper; he shall receive Ambassadors and other public Ministers; he shall take Care that the Laws be faithfully executed, and shall Commission all the Officers of the United States.

Section. 4.

The President, Vice President and all civil Officers of the United States, shall be removed from Office on Impeachment for, and Conviction of, Treason, Bribery, or other high Crimes and Misdemeanors.

Article III.

Section. 1.

The judicial Power of the United States shall be vested in one supreme Court, and in such inferior Courts as the Congress may from time to time ordain and establish. The Judges, both of the supreme and inferior Courts, shall hold their Offices during good Behaviour, and shall, at stated Times, receive for their Services a Compensation, which shall not be diminished during their Continuance in Office.

Section. 2.

The judicial Power shall extend to all Cases, in Law and Equity, arising under this Constitution, the Laws of the United States, and Treaties made, or which shall be made, under their Authority;—to all Cases affecting Ambassadors, other public Ministers and Consuls;—to all Cases of admiralty and maritime Jurisdiction;—to Controversies to which the United States shall be a Party;—to Controversies between two or more

States;— between a State and Citizens of another State;—between Citizens of different States;—between Citizens of the same State claiming Lands under Grants of different States, and between a State, or the Citizens thereof, and foreign States, Citizens or Subjects.

In all Cases affecting Ambassadors, other public Ministers and Consuls, and those in which a State shall be Party, the supreme Court shall have original Jurisdiction. In all the other Cases before mentioned, the supreme Court shall have appellate Jurisdiction, both as to Law and Fact, with such Exceptions, and under such Regulations as the Congress shall make.

The Trial of all Crimes, except in Cases of Impeachment, shall be by Jury; and such Trial shall be held in the State where the said Crimes shall have been committed; but when not committed within any State, the Trial shall be at such Place or Places as the Congress may by Law have directed.

Section. 3.

Treason against the United States, shall consist only in levying War against them, or in adhering to their Enemies, giving them Aid and Comfort. No Person shall be convicted of Treason unless on the Testimony of two Witnesses to the same overt Act, or on Confession in open Court.

The Congress shall have Power to declare the Punishment of Treason, but no Attainder of Treason shall work Corruption of Blood, or Forfeiture except during the Life of the Person attainted.

Article. IV.

Section. 1.

Full Faith and Credit shall be given in each State to the public Acts, Records, and judicial Proceedings of every other State. And the Congress may by general Laws prescribe the Manner in which such Acts, Records and Proceedings shall be proved, and the Effect thereof.

Section. 2.

The Citizens of each State shall be entitled to all Privileges and Immunities of Citizens in the several States.

A Person charged in any State with Treason, Felony, or other Crime, who shall flee from

Justice, and be found in another State, shall on Demand of the executive Authority of the State from which he fled, be delivered up, to be removed to the State having Jurisdiction of the Crime.

No Person held to Service or Labour in one State, under the Laws thereof, escaping into another, shall, in Consequence of any Law or Regulation therein, be discharged from such Service or Labour, but shall be delivered up on Claim of the Party to whom such Service or Labour may be due.

Section. 3.

New States may be admitted by the Congress into this Union; but no new State shall be formed or erected within the Jurisdiction of any other State; nor any State be formed by the Junction of two or more States, or Parts of States, without the Consent of the Legislatures of the States concerned as well as of the Congress.

The Congress shall have Power to dispose of and make all needful Rules and Regulations respecting the Territory or other Property belonging to the United States; and nothing in this Constitution shall be so construed as to Prejudice any Claims of the United States, or of any particular State.

Section. 4.

The United States shall guarantee to every State in this Union a Republican Form of Government, and shall protect each of them against Invasion; and on Application of the Legislature, or of the Executive (when the Legislature cannot be convened), against domestic Violence.

Article. V.

The Congress, whenever two thirds of both Houses shall deem it necessary, shall propose Amendments to this Constitution, or, on the Application of the Legislatures of two thirds of the several States, shall call a Convention for proposing Amendments, which, in either Case, shall be valid to all Intents and Purposes, as Part of this Constitution, when ratified by the Legislatures of three fourths of the several States, or by Conventions in three fourths thereof, as the one or the other Mode of Ratification may be proposed by the Congress; Provided that no Amendment which may be made prior to the Year One thousand eight hundred and eight shall in any Manner affect the first and fourth Clauses in the Ninth Section of the first Article; and that no State, without its Consent, shall be deprived of its equal Suffrage in the Senate.

Article. VI.

All Debts contracted and Engagements entered into, before the Adoption of this Constitution, shall be as valid against the United States under this Constitution, as under the Confederation.

This Constitution, and the Laws of the United States which shall be made in Pursuance thereof; and all Treaties made, or which shall be made, under the Authority of the United States, shall be the supreme Law of the Land; and the Judges in every State shall be bound thereby, any Thing in the Constitution or Laws of any State to the Contrary notwithstanding.

The Senators and Representatives before mentioned, and the Members of the several State Legislatures, and all executive and judicial Officers, both of the United States and of the several States, shall be bound by Oath or Affirmation, to support this Constitution; but no religious Test shall ever be required as a Qualification to any Office or public Trust under the United States.

Article. VII.

The Ratification of the Conventions of nine States, shall be sufficient for the Establishment of this Constitution between the States so ratifying the Same.

The Word, "the," being interlined between the seventh and eighth Lines of the first Page, the Word "Thirty" being partly written on an Erazure in the fifteenth Line of the first Page, The Words "is tried" being interlined between the thirty second and thirty third Lines of the first Page and the Word "the" being interlined between the forty third and forty fourth Lines of the second Page.

Attest William Jackson Secretary

Done in Convention by the Unanimous Consent of the States present the Seventeenth Day of September in the Year of our Lord one thousand seven hundred and Eighty seven and of the Independence of the United States of America the Twelfth In witness whereof We have hereunto subscribed our Names.

Presidents and their terms in office

George Washington
1789–1797

James Madison
1809–1817

John Adams
1797–1801

James Monroe
1817–1825

Thomas Jefferson
1801–1809

John Quincy Adams
1825–1829

Andrew Jackson
1829–1837

John Tyler
1841–1845

Martin Van Buren
1837–1841

James K. Polk
1845–1849

William H. Harrison
1841

Zachary Taylor
1849–1850

Millard Fillmore
1850–1853

Abraham Lincoln
1861–1865

Franklin Pierce
1853–1857

Andrew Johnson
1865–1869

James Buchanan
1857–1861

Ulysses S. Grant
1869–1877

Rutherford B. Hayes
<u>1877–1881</u>

Grover Cleveland
<u>1885–1889</u>
<u>1893–1897</u>

James A. Garfield
<u>1881</u>

Benjamin Harrison
<u>1889–1893</u>

Chester A. Arthur
<u>1881–1885</u>

William McKinley
<u>1897–1901</u>

 **Theodore Roosevelt** <u>1901–1909</u>

 **Warren G. Harding** <u>1921–1923</u>

 **William H. Taft** <u>1909–1913</u>

 **Calvin Coolidge** <u>1923–1929</u>

 **Woodrow Wilson** <u>1913–1921</u>

 **Herbert C. Hoover** <u>1929–1933</u>

Franklin Delano Roosevelt
1933–1945

John F. Kennedy
1961–1963

Harry S. Truman
1945–1953

Lyndon B. Johnson
1963–1969

Dwight D. Eisenhower
1953–1961

Richard M. Nixon
1969–1974

Gerald R. Ford
1974–1977

Ronald W. Reagan
1981–1989

Jimmy Carter
1977–1981

George H. W. Bush
1989–1993

Bill Clinton
1993–2001

George W. Bush
2001–2009

Barack Obama
2009–

CHAPTER ONE: page 4: *Lincoln Memorial*, Microsoft Corporation; page 6: *The Merchandise Of . . . Slaves, And Souls Of Men*, from "Africans on Board the Slave Bark *Wildfire*, April 30, 1860.", *Harper's Weekly*, June 2, 1860. Copyprint. Prints and Photographs Division, Library of Congress, REPRODUCTION NUMBER: LC-USZ62-19607 (1-20) ; page 9: Photo/caption from "Archiving Early America" - originally appearing in The American Gazetteer published by Jedidiah Morse in 1797, from "Historical Maps from Early America" (http:\\earlyamerica.com); page 11: United States Political Map, National Geographic, © 1996 NGS Cartographic Division.

CHAPTER TWO: page 16: *Arlington National Cemetery*, Photodisk Inc.; page 19, *No stamped paper to be had.* [*Philadelphia : Printed by Hall & Franklin, 1765*], Nov. 7, 1765, issue no. 1924, of the Pennsylvania gazette, printed at Philadelphia by David Hall and Benjamin Franklin; BOOK SOURCE: ap; vj14 06-15-98; 98-160405, Printed Ephemera Collection; Portfolio 346, Folder 45. Library of Congress, DIGITAL ID: rbpe 34604500 urn:hdl:loc.rbc/rbpe.34604500; page 21, *"Original Rough Draught of the Declaration of Independence"* from the Library of Congress; page 22, *Cornwallis* (smaller photo) from Archiving Early America, (http://www.animus.net), all rights reserved, *Surrender of Lord Cornwallis* (larger) by Trumbull, John, 1756-1843, artist., from the Detroit Publishing Company Photograph Collection , REPOSITORY, Library of Congress Prints and Photographs Division Washington, D.C. 20540 USA, DIGITAL ID (original) det 4a31167; page 25, *Macdonough's victory on Lake Champlain /* painted by H. Reinagle; engraved by B. Tanner. REPOSITORY: Library of Congress Prints and Photographs Division Washington, D.C. 20540 USA, REPRODUCTION NUMBER: LC-USZ62-63; page 27: [Sitting Bull, three-quarter-length portrait, seated, facing front, holding calumet], REPOSITORY: Library of Congress Prints and Photographs Division Washington, D.C. 20540 USA, REPRODUCTION NUMBER: LC-USZ62-12277; page 31, *Mexican War Map*, (map/caption) Microsoft Corporation; page 34, *Fort Monroe, Va. Officers of 3d Pennsylvania Heavy Artillery*, from Selected Civil War photographs, 1861-1865 (Library of Congress) REPRODUCTION NUMBER: LC-B8171-7486 DLC (b&w film neg.), Library of Congress Prints and Photographs Division Washington, D.C. 20540 USA, Digital ID: cwp 4a40120; page 35, *Auction and Negro Sales, Whitehall Street*, from Selected Civil War photographs, 1861-1865 (Library of Congress) REPRODUCTION NUMBER: LC-B8171-3608 DLC (b&w film neg.), REPOSITORY: Library of Congress Prints and Photographs Division Washington, D.C. 20540 USA, Digital ID (b&w film copy neg.): cwp 4a39949; page 36, *$200 reward*, Printed Ephemera Collection; Portfolio 86, Folder 2, COLLECTION: Broadsides, leaflets, and pamphlets from America and Europe, Digital ID: rbpe 08600200 urn:hdl:loc.rbc/rbpe; page 37, *Portrait of Maj. Gen. Ulysses S. Grant, officer of the Federal Army*, REPOSITORY: Library of Congress Prints and Photographs Division Washington, D.C. 20540 USA; Digital ID: 4a40423, *Portrait of Gen. Robert E. Lee, officer of the Confederate Army*, Washington, D.C. : Library of Congress, 1977. No. 1035 Forms part of Selected Civil War photographs, 1861-1865 (Library of

Congress) REPRODUCTION NUMBER: LC-B8172-0001 DLC (b&w film neg.) REPOSITORY: Library of Congress Prints and Photographs Division Washington, D.C. 20540 USA, Digital ID: cwp 4a40265; page 38, *District of Columbia. Company E, 4th U.S. Colored Infantry*, at Fort Lincoln, REPOSITORY Library of Congress Prints and Photographs Division Washington, D.C. 20540 USA, Digital ID: (b&w film copy neg.) cwp 4a40242, page 39: *The first reading of the Emancipation Proclamation before the cabinet*, painted by F.B. Carpenter ; engraved by A.H. Ritchie. REPRODUCTION NUMBER: LC-USZ62-2070 DLC (b&w film copy neg.) REPOSITORY: Library of Congress Prints and Photographs Division Washington, D.C. 20540 USA, Digital ID: cph 3a05802; page 40, *Reconstruction, manufactured of the best vuelta abajo tobacco*, REPRODUCTION NUMBER: LC-USZ62-90689, DIGITAL ID: cph 3b37038; page 42, *Theodore Roosevelt and the Rough Riders*, Library of Congress; page 44, *Spanish-American War Map*, (map/caption) Microsoft Corporation: page 45, William McKinley, Library of Congress; page 47, *US 7th Machine Gun Battalion, 3rd Division at Chateau Thierry bridgehead*, from Photos of the Great War - WWI Image Archive, http://www.ukans.edu/~kansite/ww_one/ photos/greatwar.htm; page 49, *Europe Before and After WWI*, Microsoft Corporation; page 50, Inauguration of President Wilson, second term, Copyright deposit; Jno. R. Idoux; March 16, 1917; DLC/PP-1917:45326. REPOSITORY: Library of Congress Prints and Photographs Division Washington, D.C. 20540 USA, Digital ID: pan 6a28173; page 53, *The Big Three*, REPRODUCTION NUMBER LC-USZ62-32833 DLC (b&w film copy neg.), REPOSITORY: Library of Congress Prints and Photographs Division Washington, D.C. 20540 USA, Digital ID: cph 3a33351; page 54, *Dwight Eisenhower*, REPRODUCTION NUMBER: LC-USZ62-25600 DLC (b&w film copy neg.) REPOSITORY: Library of Congress Prints and Photographs Division Washington, D.C. 20540 USA Digital ID: cph 3a26521; page 57, *General Douglas MacArthur*, from the MacArthur Memorial (http://sites.communitylink.org/mac/index.html); page 58, *Harry Truman*, Library of Congress; page 61, from the LBJ Digital Photo Archive; page 63, *A US Air Force (USAF) KC-135R Stratotanker, 92nd Air Refueling Wing (ARW), Fairchild Air Force Base (AFB), Washington (WA), 379th Expeditionary Air Refueling Squadron (EARS), left flanked by two Royal Air Force (RAF) GR4 Tornadoes, No. 617th Squadron, RAF Lossiemouth, United Kingdom (UK), during Operation IRAQI FREEDOM*, SSGT Suzanne M. Jenkins, USAF, jamesdale10, 2003.

CHAPTER THREE: page 72, *Mount Rushmore*, Photodisk Inc.; pages 76-79, Presidential portraits from the Library of Congress; page 80, *Md. Allan Pinkerton, President Lincoln, and Major Gen. John A. McClernand*, REPRODUCTION NUMBER: LC-B8171-7949 DLC (b&w film neg.) COLLECTION: Selected Civil War photographs, 1861-1865 (Library of Congress), REPOSITORY: Library of Congress Prints and Photographs Division Washington, D.C. 20540 USA, Digital ID: cwp 4a40264 ; page 81, *Ford Theatre*, Library of Congress; page 82, *Theodore Roosevelt*, REPRODUCTION NUMBER: LC-USZ62-13026 DLC , REPOSITORY: Library of Congress Prints and Photographs Division Washington, D.C. 20540 USA, Digital ID: cph 3a53299; page 83, *Theodore Roosevelt and John Muir*, REPRODUCTION NUMBER: LC-USZ62-107389 DLC (b&w film copy neg.) Digital ID:amrvp 3c07389; page 84, *Woodrow Wilson*, REPRODUCTION NUMBER: LC-USZ62-13028 DLC (b&w film copy neg. of cropped image) LC-

USZ62-249 DLC (b&w film copy neg.) REPOSITORY: Library of Congress Prints and Photographs Division Washington, D.C. 20540 USA DIGITAL ID: (b&w film copy neg. of cropped image) cph 3a55007, (b&w film copy neg.) cph 3a04218, page 85, *Franklin D. Roosevelt*, REPRODUCTION NUMBER: LC-USZ62-117121 DLC (b&w film copy neg. of detail), LC-USZ62-26759 DLC (b&w film copy neg.), REPOSITORY: Library of Congress Prints and Photographs Division Washington, D.C. 20540 USA, DIGITAL ID: (b&w film copy neg. of detail) cph 3c17121, (b&w film copy neg.) cph 3a27556 ; page 86, *Roosevelt Signs War Declaration*, REPRODUCTION NUMBER: LC-USZ62-15185 DLC (b&w film copy neg.), REPOSITORY: Library of Congress Prints and Photographs Division Washington, D.C. 20540 USA, DIGITAL ID: cph 3a17434; page 87, *Roosevelt's Funeral*, REPRODUCTION NUMBER: LC-USZ62-67439 DLC (b&w film copy neg.), REPOSITORY: Library of Congress Prints and Photographs Division Washington, D.C. 20540 USA DIGITAL ID: cph 3b14914.

CHAPTER FOUR: Page 92, *Statue of Liberty,* Photodisk Inc.; page 94, *Signing the Declaration of Independence*, REPRODUCTION NUMBER: LC-H8-CT-C01-062-E DLC (color corrected film copy slide), COLLECTION: Theodor Horydczak Collection (Library of Congress), REPOSITORY: Library of Congress Prints and Photographs Division Washington, D.C. 20540 USA, DIGITAL ID: thc 5a51229; page 95, *Declaration of Independence*, engraved by W.L. Ormsby, REPRODUCTION NUMBER: LC-USZ62-3736 DLC (b&w film copy neg.), LC-USZ62-56 DLC (b&w film copy neg.), REPOSITORY: Library of Congress Prints and Photographs Division Washington, D.C. 20540 USA, DIGITAL ID: cph 3a07200; page 96, *Making the Flag*, REPRODUCTION NUMBER: LC-D416-90422 DLC (b&w glass neg.) COLLECTION: Detroit Publishing Company Photograph Collection, REPOSITORY: Library of Congress Prints and Photographs Division Washington, D.C. 20540 USA, DIGITAL ID: det 4a26653; page 97, *Constitution of the United States*, from the National Archives and Records Administration; page 99, *Capitol Hill,* Microsoft Corporation.

CHAPTER FIVE: page 108, *Washington Monument*, Washington Monument Photo Gallery; page 110, *Eisenhower*, REPRODUCTION NUMBER: LC-USZ62-84331 DLC (b&w film copy neg.) REPOSITORY: Library of Congress Prints and Photographs Division Washington, D.C. 20540 USA DIGITAL ID: cph 3b30902; page 112, *Telephone Operators, 1952,* Seattle Municipal Archives from Seattle, WA; page 113, John F. Kennedy presidential portrait from the Library of Congess; page 114, *Johnson takes the Oath*, from the LBJ Digital Photo Archive, by Cecil Stoughton; page 115, *Civil Rights Act of 1964*, from the LBJ Digital Photo Archive; page 117, Kissinger, Nixon, Ford, Haig, from the Gerald Ford Library; page 119, *Ronald Reagan* (source unknown), caption Microsoft Corporation; page 120, President Ronald Reagan and Vice President George Bush at the 1984 Republican National Convention in Dallas, Texas, August 23, 1984. Reagan Library Archives; page 122, *Bill Clinton*, Michigan State University, caption Microsoft Corporation; page 123, Barack Obama, realjameso16.